A Guide for Beginning Elementary Teachers

A Guide for Beginning Elementary Teachers

Getting Hired and Staying Inspired . . .

Donna M. Donoghue
Sally Wakefield
Esther Collins

Teacher Ideas Press
Portsmouth, NH

Teacher Ideas Press
A division of Reed Elsevier Inc.
361 Hanover Street
Portsmouth, NH 03801–3912
www.teacherideaspress.com

Offices and agents throughout the world

© 2005 by Donna M. Donoghue

Library of Congress Cataloging-in-Publication Data

Donoghue, Donna.
A guide for beginning elementary teachers : getting hired and staying inspired / by Donna Donoghue, Sally Wakefield, Esther Collins.
p. cm.
ISBN 1-59469-005-7 (alk. paper)
1. Elementary school teaching—Vocational guidance—United States—Handbooks, manuals, etc. 2. Elementary school teachers—Employment—United States—Handbooks, manuals, etc. 3. First year teachers—United States—Handbooks, manuals, etc. I. Wakefield, Sally. II. Collins, Esther. III. Title.
LB1776.2.D66 2005
370'.23'73—dc22
2004006617

Editor: Suzanne Barchers
Production Coordinator: Angela Rice
Typesetter: Westchester Book Services
Cover Design: Anne Payne
Manufacturing: Steve Bernier

Printed in the United States of America on acid-free paper

09 08 07 06 05 ML 1 2 3 4 5

We dedicate this book to the many hardworking, caring teachers everywhere in appreciation for all that they do, and in hope that it will help make their jobs a little easier.

Contents

1

Getting Hired as an Elementary Teacher

Congratulations! You have just graduated or are about to graduate from college with a degree in elementary education. What comes next? The answer to this question may be the biggest challenge of all—finding a teaching job in a location in which you would like to live, work, and play. This chapter breaks down the job-search process and details it in easy-to-read sections, helping you become more acquainted with the course of action you need to take.

Deciding Where You Want to Live

One of the most important things you need to decide is where you would like to live. Ideally, you have thought about this at some time before now. If you have, then you most likely have a good idea of the area in which you would like to live and work. If you haven't made this decision, then stop and ask yourself some very important questions:

- Do I want to be near my family?

- Would I rather be away and on my own?

- Should I move back to where I used to live or look for a job in a completely new area?

- Do I have good friends whom I want to be near?

- When and where should I look for an apartment or home?

Try to answer these questions honestly, without being influenced by anyone else. Being unhappy with your location can make or break your satisfaction with your teaching career.

Some people enjoy being close to family to be able to participate in family activities and affairs. If you have siblings, parents, or relatives whom you would like to stay in close contact with, then it would probably be good for you to look for a teaching position near them. Another reason to be located near your family is to have a support system for any situation that might come up. Without close friends nearby, it is sometimes difficult to face certain situations alone.

Then there are those who have dreamed of being away and entirely on their own right out of college. This is fine if you have been independent while attending college and do not feel the need for as much family involvement. Perhaps you have imagined living in a certain place and want to try it. This is quite all right if you have thoroughly thought it out and feel that you can handle whatever comes up by yourself. Teaching school can be stressful at times, so be sure to befriend another teacher or person whom you can lean on in tough times.

Another consideration that will influence where you look for a teaching position is the cost of living. There is great variation in the cost of living throughout the country. While you are searching for a place to live, be sure to give this factor some thought. Teachers' salaries are notoriously low, and you must factor this in the cost of living for your desired location. In other words, ask yourself, "Will I make enough money teaching in this community to live comfortably?" You may check the cost of living on the Web site for the area that you are considering. Check a real estate site for house and apartment prices in that area. Some young teachers who are just starting out find that having another person live with them and help share the costs of an apartment helps. Later, when you become more comfortable financially, you can go out on your own.

Wherever you decide to locate, be sure to have a good reason for going there. Think it through thoroughly before you try to find a job in that location. You might want to consider the socioeconomic, ethnic, and language background of that community before you make your decision. Your future happiness can depend on your choice.

Preparing Your Resume and Portfolio

If you have not yet typed up a resume, now is a good time to do this because you will need to send them out to schools with vacancies and/or bring one to any interview you have. You might consider this a difficult task because you most likely have not had much experience in the teaching field. Do not despair! Employers will be looking for a resume that is prepared in a recognizable, easy-to-read format. They will be looking for any experiences and leadership positions that you held while you were an undergraduate. So think about your college career and write down everything in which you participated. Be sure to include any clubs, organizations, and community service projects in which you participated or held a leadership position. Also, write down any honors or awards that you received during your college or high school years. Remember to include any committees you served on or any important research projects you might have completed. Be sure to indicate your major and any minor subjects, the kind of degree that you have or will earn, and the date that you received or expect to receive it. If you worked while attending college, state your position and your job description, or what was expected of you.

You can locate many Web sites to assist you with your resume, or you can purchase a software program to help you. There are many great programs available for just this purpose. It would be worthwhile to invest in one if you do not have the latest information on resume writing. You will want a resume that promotes you in the best way.

Many universities and colleges require that students who are studying to be teachers keep a portfolio of their accomplishments while in school. Most of the courses that you will be taking or have taken ask that you complete a term paper or a project at the end of each course. You will most likely spend a semester or two in a school classroom, either as an observer or as an intern teacher. Save all of the items you created while in the classroom. Also, save an example of any ideas that you got from a supervising teacher and keep copies of work, learning games, or projects that your students completed. Photograph these projects or activities. Then, arrange these photographs and other items according to grade level or subject area and put them in a large portfolio packet or folder. Use clear plastic cover sheets to protect them, if possible.

Interviewers often ask to see portfolios. Offer to let them browse through yours. It can tell them a lot about your organizational skills and also give them insight into your creative abilities. If you are technologically savvy, you might even be able to create a video or DVD of your intern experiences.

Finding the Vacancies

Where can you look to find a teaching position that is suited to your major strengths? If you have any teacher friends, you can start by networking with them. Another thing to do is ask about vacancies at the district school board office where you live or would like to work. Find out if the schools are run by the county, city, or certain districts, as many of them are. Call the school board or superintendent's office and ask to speak to someone in the personnel department who is in charge of hiring new teachers. Be sure to ask the name of that person in case you need to call again in the future. It's nice to deal with one person who may become familiar with your inquiries, and, by speaking with the same person each time, you won't have to start all over again with every phone call. Have your questions thought out and written down so that you can get them answered satisfactorily. The following are some questions that you might ask:

- May I please ask your name?

- What positions are available?

- Where will these be located?

- Do you know what grade levels they might be?

- May I ask what the salary is for a beginning teacher in this district?

- Who would be the contact person for an interview for this position?

- If I should have any further questions, may I ask for your help again?

Be polite and thank the person for the information, making sure to use the person's name before ending the conversation.

The next step is to make a telephone call to the principal or other administrator to set up an interview. Be careful not to call during the opening or closing time of school because administrators are usually busiest during that time. Always begin the conversation by stating your name and the purpose of your call. Be polite, call the person by name, and set up a time that is convenient for the interviewing person or group. You need to make yourself available according to their schedules. Remember, they are the ones who are working! You would be surprised how much of an impression your telephone conversation can make. A polite voice with a positive note can make the difference between getting the interview or not.

Preparing for the Interview

You want everything to be as perfect as possible in your interview, so you will need to prepare. The first thing you should do is write the date and time of your interview on your calendar. Be sure to be on time for this important event. When the interview day arrives, leave early and give yourself time in case of traffic tie-ups or other unforeseen delays. You need to be calm and focused during this occasion.

Being granted an interview by a school or district is an indication that they have openings available. The most important part begins now. You must convince the interviewer that you are the best one for the job. There may be a team of people who are present for your interview, so be prepared to sit and answer questions in front of a group. This takes time and some investigative work on your part.

Here are some steps to take before an interview:

- Take the time to research the school or school system for which you will be interviewing. Find out as much as you can about the history of the community, the school, and its location. Check on the populations, the programs offered, and the philosophy of the school. Take a drive to find the exact location of the place where you are expected to interview and note how long it takes to get there. Notice where visitors' parking is permitted. Plan to arrive fifteen minutes before you are scheduled to meet and never keep your interviewers waiting.

- Plan ahead for the proper clothing to wear to your interview. Because you are a professional, it is important that your attire conveys the proper demeanor. Avoid flashy clothes that may distract from you and your qualification for the position. Most important, make sure you are comfortable. Your interview is not the place to break in new shoes or to try a new look. The more comfortable you are, the more confident you will appear.

- Plan to bring several (4–6) resumes to your interview, one for the principal in case he or she doesn't have it in front of him or her and a few extras in case the principal asks the vice-principal or team you might be working with to sit in on the interview.

- Always prepare for the types of questions you may be asked in an interview. In most cases, the questions will be of a behavioral nature, such as "Explain a time when you were forced to deal with a difficult situation." Keep your answers direct and provide detail, but avoid rambling. Many interviewers use the STAR method (situation, task, action, and results) as a model to answer most behavioral questions.

- If you have friends who have had interviews before, you might ask them what kinds of questions they were asked. Glean from them any awkward or unusual situations they encountered during an interview. Think about those situations and how you might handle them if something similar happened to you. The more you prepare mentally, the more at ease you will feel in any situation.

- If you don't know the answer to a question or don't understand it, then ask to have it rephrased or simply say that you are not familiar with that topic. It's better to admit that you don't know the answer than to answer it incorrectly. It is fine to say, "I haven't really had any experience in that area yet, but I would be glad to work on it."

A frequently asked question is, "What is your philosophy of teaching?" Be prepared to answer such a question, even though it is a very broad one. Your honest answer will give the interviewer some insight as to what kind of a teacher you would be. In answering a question such as this, you should include your ideas on classroom discipline, some basic instructional strategies, and your vision of a classroom in which teacher and students have mutual respect.

Making good eye contact with your interviewer(s) is important. Also, use good posture and smile often to project a great attitude. These things will set the tone for the meeting. Experiencing a positive interview helps build your confidence to face another one later. It won't be long before you land the teaching position that is perfectly suited to you.

After each interview, be sure to thank your hosts with a small note. One trick is to prepare the envelope and a general paragraph ahead of time. After the interview, write a second paragraph in more detail. Be sure to reiterate your interest in the job and consider highlighting a quick reason or two why you are a good fit for the position. Mail the card that day.

Interview Tips

Here are some helpful tips to keep in mind for your interview:

DO	DON'T
Dress professionally.	Wear flashy or inappropriate clothes.
Maintain good eye contact.	Chew gum.
Use a firm and confident handshake.	Ramble or talk excessively.
Have five selling points about yourself.	Be afraid to answer, "I don't know."
Be enthusiastic (smile often).	Forget your interviewer's name.
Stay focused.	Be late.
Be a good listener.	Talk salary.
Contribute constructive comments.	
Send a card to thank your hosts.	

Reviewing the Contract

After you have landed the teaching position of your dreams and have accepted it, you then enter the contract phase. A contract is simply an agreement between two parties. There are many different policies and issues in each contract, so before you sign on the dotted line be sure you know what you are agreeing to. In other words, read over your contract carefully—know what it entails and be sure that you agree with it. If you have any questions, call the principal or someone in the personnel office to have them answered. If the contract needs to be changed, now is the time to negotiate the change. Call someone in charge and talk it over. Perhaps you need more flexible hours on a certain day. In this case, you could ask if it would be all right to stay later another day to make up the time. There may be other alternatives that your principal might consider. Just explain your circumstances; if they are honest and necessary, the principal might be able to make arrangements to help you out.

Some school districts provide annual contracts to teachers. This means you are served a new contract every year that you teach, providing you have met the district's standards and they would like you to return the next year. Other school districts put new teachers on an annual contract until they have proven themselves or until they have performed satisfactorily for a certain number of years.

At that time, they are given a continuing contract that is effective until either party wishes to break it.

Regardless of the kind contract you are offered, be certain you understand and agree with its contents before signing. It takes two satisfied participants to make a contract workable. By signing it, you are telling the employer that you are willing to abide by the regulations set forth in the agreement.

2

Things You Can Do Before School Begins

You've just signed your contract, and you're excited! There are so many ideas popping into your head about your classroom, its centers, your teaching techniques, and so on. Your mind seems to be going a hundred miles an hour. You are probably asking yourself, "What do I do now, and how do I get started?" If you are an organized person, you might like to get a jump on the upcoming school year by laying some groundwork over the summer.

If possible, visit your school to familiarize yourself with its layout. Check out your classroom and see how many bulletin boards, walls, and windows it has. This will give you an idea of what you have to work around so that you can use each space to its full potential. If you have a lot of bulletin boards, you could have one for writing, another for math, and so forth. You might make your bulletin boards into learning tools. For example, one could be a center for writing. You could have several activities planned for different times of the year (see Chapter 3 for center ideas).

If you know what you would like to do, work on it over the summer when you have some time. You might even ask your principal if it would be possible to get into your classroom early to put some of your bulletin boards up. When the teachers report for their first week, you may be shocked by the number of meetings held regarding policies, curriculum, and scheduling. You may be hard-pressed to get a lot done in your room. If you can organize over the summer what you want to do and have it up or ready to put up, you will be in good shape. Then you can pace yourself accordingly.

Check the layout of furniture in your classroom. This will help you plan your seating and center arrangement. You might consider having your students sit in rows or in groups. Until you have established your routine, you might want to consider keeping desks in rows. The classroom layout also gives you some ideas for placing bookcases, project tables, textbooks, and media and computer centers, as well as your desk and personal planning area.

Getting to Know Your Principal and Support Staff

The first thing you should do as a new teacher is get to know your principal. It is important to have a principal with whom you can talk and who will support you when a problem arises in your classroom.

Learn a few things about your principal's personal likes, dislikes, and family. This small talk enables you to have a brief, friendly conversation about everyday life and helps you establish a positive rapport and develop a good relationship with your principal. Mutual trust and understanding between a principal and a teacher is essential for a successful working relationship.

Most likely the principal will introduce you to the office staff. Make sure you become friends with the secretary, who is very important to the operation of the school. The secretary can almost instantly locate any information you might need. It would be a good idea to do something nice for the secretary on the first day of school. The office can be a hectic place, with late registrations, new teachers, returning staff, and so on. Bring a single rose or a candy bar to put on the secretary's desk, along with a cheery note. You can be assured that it will be appreciated and remembered.

Many times the guidance counselor, food service people, and other support staff start work early in the school year. Try to meet these people and introduce yourself ahead of time. Also, get to know the custodians; they will be a great help during the first days of school, assisting with transporting items to and from your classroom, as well as moving larger items within your room.

Meeting with Team Teachers

It's good to make contact with your team during the summer, either by phone or a lunch meeting, for many reasons:

- *Personality*—You show yourself to be a friendly and outgoing person, and you get a chance to see what your coteachers' personalities are like.

- *Clarification*—You can use the opportunity to ask questions or clear up any uncertainties.

- *Brainstorming*—The team can discuss ideas they may have concerning your curriculum, or you can use your team as a sounding board for ideas that you have.

- *Experience*—Your team can provide a wealth of information from their combined experiences. They can inform you about the types of items the school will provide and what you may need to purchase. If you plan to have centers, ask them what materials are provided for this purpose.

- *Preparation*—Spending time with any member of your team before school starts will save you time and help you focus on what to expect. Ask what units you will be teaching the first months of school in different subject areas. This way, if you are planning a bulletin board, you will know what to purchase.

Don't be timid about making the first move. Most school staff members are thrilled to make a new teacher's acquaintance and want to be helpful. You need not be afraid to ask for help. Chances are there will be one or more members of your team who will make you feel comfortable. Start with these teachers, and you will be fine. It's easier to be successful when you're with friendly people.

Visiting Your Local Educational Supply Store

After you have had a chance to visit your school and have gotten suggestions from some people on your team, you can start planning. Go to your local educational supply store and check it out. If you do not have one in your area, ask the school secretary if you can borrow some educational supply books from the school. Also, ask the principal or secretary if you can have a purchase order for the things you will need for your classroom. Each teacher is usually allotted a certain amount of money from the school budget for classroom supplies. Find out how much money you are allowed, and keep in mind that this amount will have to last the entire year. Ask about the policy for classroom spending, since each school's policy is different.

Educational stores have many shortcuts that will save you time. You can find ideas for unit studies, bulletin boards, centers, cutouts, and much more. It is a good idea to have bulletin board and unit-study items laminated. Check with your school to see if they will do that for you. If your school does not have a laminating machine, many educational stores will do it for an extra cost. It is well worth the investment, since your bulletin board items will last for years.

Other great venues for procuring materials include discount stores and garage sales. Many times you can find great buys on puzzles, games, furniture, and other materials for your classroom. You can also ask friends and relatives to get involved and give them a list of needed things.

Setting Up a Classroom That Works for You

By now you probably know how you want your classroom to look and function. You may want to give some consideration to centers. If you plan to use centers in your classroom, you can easily work on them during the summer. (See Chapter 3, for more information about centers.) You could have some centers prepared and ready to be quickly set up in your classroom when school starts. Think ahead about which materials and furniture you need for each center. Using your time wisely in the summer can help you save time during the first busy weeks of school.

Organizing Closet Space

Ideally, you will have at least one good-sized closet or cabinet in your classroom. If you can, check it out for any supplies that might be left over from the year before. Take an inventory of supplies you have, so you will know what you need. Rearrange the closet or cabinet so it is user-friendly. You might put all the art supplies and paper together, then arrange an area for school supplies, such as paper clips, tape, markers, pens, and so on. Leave some space for your bulletin board items, games, and any teaching tools you might have.

If you are fortunate enough to have more than one closet or cabinet, place the items you will need most often in the closet or cabinet closest to your work area. This convenience will save you time throughout the year.

Many new schools have a separate office in which a teacher may plan and organize lessons. It would be wise to keep the supplies you need for planning in that room, so they will be readily available. Good organization is the key to success.

Planning for Bulletin Boards

If you are able to see your classroom before school starts, you can start thinking about the kinds of bulletin boards that would best serve both you and your students. Once school starts, it is very difficult to find the time to work on things like this, so think ahead.

Your first task once you are in your room is to count the number of bulletin boards and to measure each one. If you have time at this point, it will be helpful to pick a color theme for your classroom. Using the colors that you have chosen, cover each bulletin board with craft paper. This kind of paper, also called butcher paper, comes in large rolls, and is used to cover large work areas. You might ask if your school has any rolls of craft paper that you can use. If they do not, then ordinary construction paper will do. Some teachers even purchase cloth to cover their boards. Whatever you do, choose a color that will best show off your students' work. Yellow is a cheerful color that does not fade, and other colors show up nicely on it. Blues tend to fade throughout the year. Red also fades but not as much as blue. Cut and staple on the background color so that the boards are ready for your first official day. If you do not have any ready-made bulletin board borders, then visit your local educational supply store. Be sure to buy enough to cover the perimeter of all of your boards.

When you visit the school supply store, be sure to check out their ready-made bulletin boards. Numerous companies manufacture these in delightful colors and pictures. Purchase ready-made boards in general topics, so you know you can use them, being careful not to spend your money on something not covered in your curriculum. Often, school districts or book publishers provide teachers with posters and other resources, many of which are nice enough to put up on bulletin boards.

Save some bulletin board space for your students' work. They love seeing their work displayed, and doing so gives them a sense of pride and ownership in their classroom.

Try to have bulletin boards that don't require constant changing. Many of them can stay up indefinitely, especially if they don't have a seasonal theme. The following ideas can be used for your classroom bulletin boards:

1. *Daily Math Bulletin Board*—A daily math board is made up of charts depicting the math we use in our day-to-day life, including a calendar, a tally chart, a place value chart, a counting to 100 chart, and charts depicting money and a clock face. On the first day of school you teach the number 1 on your board: 1 day on the calendar, 1 tally on the chart, 1 straw for place value in the ones place, 1 penny on the money chart, and so on. On the second day, teach the number 2. Each day you can build on this and do exchanges such as 5 pennies is the same as 1 nickel, for every fifth tally you cross over, 10 straws moves from the ones place to the tens place, and so on. Add 1 each day on the math board and review each of these strategies each day. It takes only minutes to do and yet reviews strategies that are used in everyday life.

   • *Calendar*—Have this located near the front of the room. Some teachers prefer pocket-chart calendars, which allow you to simply change the month and insert the days in the proper order. You can also put translucent colored plastic squares over the calendar days to make a pattern.

   • *Hundred Days Chart*—This is nice to have up all year to refer to when teaching or reviewing odd and even numbers and skip counting. With this chart, you can count the number of days you are in school and use this number for all of the following charts:

   • *Place Value Chart*—This chart shows ones, tens, and hundreds. It can be handmade with paper cups and straws, or it can be purchased.

   • *Tally Chart*—Use a long piece of ticker tape on the bulletin board to count the number of days of school. The students will have fun counting by fives and predicting when the next crossover will happen.

   • *Money Chart*—With this chart, students learn to use pennies and trade for a nickel, dime, and quarter. If you teach older students, they can find out the number of different ways to make change.

   • *Clock*—Put a clear plastic laminate or plastic sleeve over a poster that has the face of a clock on it. With erasable pens in different colors, mark one minute for each day of school. Use red for the first five minutes, black for the next five minutes, and alternate colors for each five minute interval. This helps students understand that there are five minutes between each number on the clock face. When you are ready to teach telling time, the students will quickly learn how to skip-count by fives. When sixty minutes is reached, explain to the students that they have reached one hour. Then erase the pen and start over, repeating the activity once again. You might also have the students write the time beneath the clock.

2. *Birthday Bulletin Board*—Young children love to have their names on a birthday board during the month of their birthday.

3. *Safety Bulletin Board*—This is an excellent bulletin board for the beginning and end of the year. The American Automobile Association (AAA) produces large, colorful posters, designed by children that illustrate different safety rules.

4. *Rules or Expected Behaviors Chart*—Rules should be posted somewhere prominently in the classroom.

5. *Classroom Jobs Bulletin Board*—It's nice to have the students involved in the everyday happenings. To save yourself time, have the jobs listed with colorful pockets under each one. Make strips shaped like bookmarks from tagboard or used file folders. Type or write each student's name at the top of a strip. At the beginning of each week, you can easily assign jobs to different students. Be sure that you rotate all students equally. Some teachers call this their Helping Hands bulletin board. (See list of possible classroom jobs in the next section of this chapter.)

6. *Working Bulletin Boards*—Use a variety of pocket charts of various types to create a learning center on a bulletin board. For example, for language arts, you might use pocket charts for teaching and reviewing synonyms, antonyms, homophones, sequencing, classifying, word families, ABC order, and short and long vowels. For science, you might review the parts of a plant or the names of the planets in the solar system. For social studies, students can match a capital city to its state. This is a great idea to help reinforce what you have taught your students.

7. *Patterning Chart*—Pocket charts also allow you to teach patterns. You can buy pattern squares from an educational store with a variety of patterns. Patterns are a fun challenge for students.

8. *Wire Hangings*—Another idea is to have certain class projects, such as maps, drawings, or stories, hung up around the edge of the room on a strip of wire or string. Have your custodian help you install the wire first. Then it will be available to you for the remainder of the year.

9. *Store Displays*—Check department stores and those that sell back-to-school apparel and supplies for unused displays. Often, they have posters or banners that they will gladly give away after the rush of back-to-school purchasing is over.

Having colorful and functional bulletin boards in your classroom will give it a pleasant atmosphere and will make your students proud to be a member of your class. Parents will also be impressed with your creative and colorful bulletin boards. A nice environment is important for a positive attitude, and the appearance of your classroom plays a big part in this.

Classroom Jobs

A list of classroom jobs can be posted in your classroom. The following are common classroom jobs:

Team Leader—Passes out and collects papers.

Calendar Helper—Puts the correct date on the calendar and leads the math activity board with place value and money using today's date for the number.

Messenger—Brings attendance to the office and the lunch count to the cafeteria.

Clock Watcher—Helps remind the teacher a couple of minutes before lunch, gym (P.E.), art, and other special classes.

Drink Counter—Ensures each student gets ten seconds for a drink at the water fountain after P.E.

Line Leaders—Leads the line and is also the bathroom monitor (be sure to select a boy and a girl to monitor bathrooms).

Homework Folder Helper—Takes out homework, adds new homework, checks to make sure homework is complete, marks the homework chart.

Super Clean Team—Stacks chairs, helps pass the garbage cans around when needed, checks sink area to make sure it is clean.

Red Cross Helper—Walks students who are sick or injured down to the health room or designated location.

City Commissioner—Helps run class meetings. During the meeting the class may share +s (all the positive things noted in the classroom that day). Deltas (negative things or happenings) can also be noted and discussed along with ideas to help the next day go smoother, including changes in behavior and better ways to do activities.

Writer's Workshop Monitor—Helps keep students on task during sharing time.

Library Committee—Reminds students of their library day, keeps the library clean and organized, ensures students put the library books away correctly.

Setting Up Good Organization Systems

Filing

Organizing a good filing system is of utmost importance in the teaching field, just as it is in any kind of professional work. Knowing that you have a worksheet for a certain subject or skill but not being able to locate it can be very frustrating. If you start with a filing plan in mind and stick to it, you will be ahead of the game. The amount of papers that a teacher has to handle throughout a school year can become overwhelming if you fail to stick to your plan.

Most classroom teachers are provided with at least one metal filing cabinet. If you do not have a cabinet at your disposal, then request one from your principal. A four-drawer cabinet is best, but until you get one you can purchase and use plastic bins made for hanging files or file boxes. Use a file cabinet drawer, or one plastic bin or box, for each subject, if possible.

Here are some tips to help you form an organizational plan from the start:

· For packing away any used activity sheets, manila file folders are the best way to preserve them for future use. Have a sturdy plastic bin or crate with hanging file folders near your work area in which to put all used worksheets. Have these hanging files labeled according to subject area so that the activity sheets can be quickly filed in the proper place.

· Take at least one day a week to file all the used worksheets and any overhead transparencies, maps, puzzles, and other materials into their permanent file cabinet drawer. Be sure that each file folder is labeled correctly and that you file the folders according to subject area.

· Type easy-to-read labels on all of your files. It's much easier to find exactly what you are looking for if you can read the label.

· Throw away any excess papers that you will not need. Your desk can easily become cluttered with unnecessary papers. Getting rid of them will help you stay organized.

· Label each file cabinet drawer with the exact subject that it holds. Inside the drawers use tall, labeled dividers to separate the different skills. For example, in the file drawer labeled "Writing Skills," you might have several tall dividers, or markers, to separate the following files:

Sentence Development

Paragraph Composition

Letter Writing

Quotations

Expository Writing

Narrative Writing

Persuasive Writing

Report Writing

Functional Writing

If you are fortunate enough to have a classroom aide, instructing the aide in proper filing and labeling can be a great time-saver. You must trust your aide to file materials correctly, however. Most teachers do not have an aide to do this kind of work. If you're like most teachers, a competent and dependable volunteer could type your file labels for you.

For certain subjects, such as science and social studies, a file box may be a better choice for a filing system because it can hold maps, posters, and other bulky materials. Some teachers prefer a large three-ring binder to hold worksheets related to a certain subject, such as math or writing. You can put overhead transparencies inside clear plastic page protectors to keep them from any damage or fading.

No matter which kind of filing system you choose, you will find it to be your best ally in the teaching profession. Keeping it properly organized will be a challenge unless you discipline yourself to work on it once a week. The unfiled material can quickly mount up and become a daunting pile if you leave it unfiled. Finally, having your files neatly put away at the end of the year will help you tremendously the next fall.

Storage

Storage is a major problem for teachers, especially those who teach the lower elementary grades where the children work with so many types of manipulatives. Many teachers opt to buy plastic stackable drawers that pull out from the front, to allow for easy access. To save time during the first week of school, ask a parent or volunteer to take home the manipulatives you will need the most and sort them into plastic bags. Then have them put the bags into their designated drawers. This will keep your classroom neat. (*Note:* If you need tips on organizing the manipulatives for your particular grade level, ask a member of your team for guidance.) Stackable drawers are also useful for centers. You might have a writing center in one drawer; pattern blocks in another, an art box for card making in another, and so on.

Teacher's Desk Area

A good classroom setup should include an area set aside for the teacher's needs. In many of the newly constructed schools, there is a separate teacher's office and planning area. If you have one of those, all you need to do is arrange the furniture and start setting up your files. If you are not so fortunate, you will need to provide a space for yourself within the classroom boundary. Search for an area that is slightly removed from most of the activities of the classroom. A corner of the room at the front or back usually works very well for this space. Having your space near the front of the room allows you to be near the TV and other media equipment that often need your attention. Having your area face the classroom door also helps you see who is coming into or leaving your room. Most important, be sure that this area provides you with a good overall view of what is going on in your classroom.

Once you have chosen the location of the teacher's area, the next thing to do is move all of the furniture and other items that you will need to that area. Every teacher needs a nice desk and comfortable chair, so try to find a chair that is comfortable for you. Select one that also allows you to pull yourself up to your desk at the right height to read and write. Most teachers find it necessary to have a sturdy bookshelf on which to put all of their books and resource materials. A good place to have this shelf is directly behind the desk area. Place your filing cabinet nearby because you will need it for your lesson planning. Some teachers prefer to have another long table placed perpendicular to their desk to extend the surface area for their use. Under this table you could place any temporary crates or filing bins that hold upcoming or used lesson files. The use of the rest of the area is up to you. Some teachers find that having another adult chair in that space is convenient. Others find that having a teacher's bulletin board nearby is handy for posting important notices. Having an inbox and outbox located nearby might also prove useful.

However you arrange your personal space is up to you. The goal is to have it be convenient. Make sure that the children know that this is *your* area and that they are not to go into that area unless you ask them to. Having it set up according to your needs and comfort will allow you to spend many hours there planning and reviewing your students' work.

Furniture Arrangement

Teachers should give considerable thought as to how they would like their classroom set up. You want it to be teacher-, student-, parent-, and volunteer-friendly. In other words, it should be functional and inviting.

Here are some suggested items for the front of your classroom:

- *Classroom Schedule and Rules*—This allows parents to view schedules and events quickly. Also, having the classroom rules displayed is very important because they are a visible reminder of student expectations.

- *Overhead Projector*—Be sure to organize your cart with your entire overhead teaching necessities and check the placement of the projection on your screen.

- *Television and VCR*—Place these in an area where students can see them. Usually in front, off to the side, is preferable.

- *American Flag*—Place high on the wall in front of the classroom.

- *Pocket Chart*—Sentence strips or vocabulary that will be used during a lesson are placed in the chart.

- *Behavior Chart*—Many teachers have a chart that is used for noting students' positive behavior or privileges lost by students who do not adhere to the rules.

- *Furniture*—A small table or desk near the door is an ideal place to put notices or bulletins that need to go home. You will also need a table for the students' projects, one that can be used as well for volunteers who work with students.

- *Emergency Information*—A student roster with emergency procedures should be placed by the door where you can reach it quickly for drills or emergencies. (*Tip:* Glue the roster inside a manila folder. Put a tacky strip on the back of the folder and a strip on the wall next to the door. Stick the folder to the wall using the tacky strip.)

Make good use of the sides of your room. If you don't have built-in bookcases, decide where you need to place some for the most effective use. For example, you might want one behind your reading group table, so you can use it for organizing your reading materials.

You will need a bookcase for your teacher's manuals, materials, and resources. Many teachers put a bookcase behind their desk, so these materials are handy during lesson plan writing. You will need a place, perhaps a bookcase, for the students to keep their lunch boxes. If your classroom has a sink, locate the lunch boxes close to it in case of a leaking thermos or other spill. A sink nearby enables students to wash their hands and pick up their lunches quickly.

The walls above the bookcases can be used for your classroom goals, a word wall for vocabulary, or any other items you deem necessary. Be choosy what you display on your walls. You want your classroom to be tastefully filled with positive goals, expectations, and students' work.

Classroom Library

To set up your classroom library, you will need a bookcase placed in an area where the students can have easy access to it and you can monitor it. Do not place it too close to an instructional area, as it can be distracting. If you are a new teacher and your classroom library has not been established, don't panic. There are resources available to you. Go to your school's library and ask the librarian if she can give you some books to get started. Contact teachers in the school who might have extra books you could have or use. Visit your local county library also. Many county libraries allow educators to check out books and resources. Some libraries will even deliver the books once a month to your school librarian to distribute and collect. All you have to do is call and tell them the types of books you want or whatever your needs are. Also, don't forget that parents are a great resource for books children have outgrown. Put a want ad in your school paper for books that parents would like to contribute to the school. Many book clubs, though they promote books to be bought by the students, offer bargain books at excellent prices to teachers. The PTA might be able to help you with funding, or you can write a proposal for school improvement funds. There are also grants available for this purpose.

Your library should be comfortable for the students. You might ask the students to bring some pillows to give it an inviting look. Set up the rules for the library and a type of system to check out books. (See Library Checkout form, Form 2.1, at the end of this chapter.) A simple checkout sheet on a clipboard will do. Many teachers mark their books or bookshelves with different colored dots, indicating the reading level. This helps the students easily find books on their level. You could even put the dots somewhere on the books, so the students can put them back where they belong.

Computer Center

Decide which area in your classroom will work best for your computer center. Many teachers prefer the back of the classroom, so that it does not interfere with their teaching. If you intend to have students work at the computer while you continue to teach, set up the area so that you can keep an eye on the students. Computers, printers, and monitors need a lot of room, so plan this area carefully.

Student Seating

With the space you have remaining, the main decision will be how to set up your students' desks. Many teachers like putting desks in clusters of four and five. This saves space in a small classroom, and provides a seating arrangement that is more conducive to group work and cooperative learning. Other teachers prefer two students sitting side-by-side in rows. The idea behind this is to put a strong student with a struggling student for extra help as well as a peer model for success. Still, other teachers like to have a lot of discussion and sharing among their students and might enjoy the U shape for desks. Finally, some teachers feel that they have more control and that students will work more independently if students are in rows, one behind the other. The choice is a very personal one and is decided according to each teacher's needs and teaching style.

Special Seating

If a child has an eye problem or is not hearing well, seat him or her in the front of the room. Many children with hearing loss can read lips, so make sure the child is seated where he or she can follow your lips as you turn toward the board or explain a chart in the front of the room. Take into consideration whether you teach from the right or from the left of the board.

It is helpful to visit your students' prior classroom teachers for a few minutes before school starts and ask if there is a child who is unusually small or large. Petite students need to be placed in the front of the room, while taller ones can be at the side or in back.

If you know ahead of time that you have students who could be problems or have attention disorders, it is helpful to seat them where you can easily get them back on track so that they don't disrupt the other students.

Many schools have teachers fill out some type of informational form about their students at the end of the year. These forms can give you an idea of what to expect—specifically, students with short attention spans, focus problems, vision or hearing loss, or unusual height for the age group. These will be your clues in creating your classroom seating.

Learning from a Classroom That Works for You

If you follow these ideas in this chapter for setting up a classroom, you will be off to a great start. As you get to know your students in the following weeks, you can experiment with other ways to change or improve on your classroom setup.

At the end of the school year, you can design a map of your classroom that shows the way you would like it to be set up when you return from summer vacation. Post it on the blackboard so that the custodians can view it and know what you expect. On your map, show where you want different items set up, for example, your desk, bookcases, a reading table, students' desks, chairs, overhead projectors, computers, and so forth. The custodians will be able not only to clean your room, but also to set it up the way you want it, saving you precious time when you return in the fall.

As you go along, keep notes on what works and what doesn't work. Don't expect your room organization to be perfect at first. This takes time and experience. Strive to make it workable until you know your preferences. If your room is well organized, your students will know how to help you pass out materials and how to replace them correctly. An organized classroom will also allow your lessons to run more smoothly, and you will have more time for instruction. It pays to give a lot of thought to the organization of your classroom, with the ultimate goal of making it teacher-, student-, parent-, and volunteer-friendly.

Form 2.1

Library Checkout

Name	Book	Check-Out	Check-In

3

Starting the School Year Successfully

Getting Started

Your room is ready, and the first day is here. You have given a lot of thought to how you wanted your room set up. Now is the time to think about how you want to run your classroom. For this, routines and procedures are essential. Procedure is what the teacher wants his or her students to do. Routine is what the students should know to do automatically, without being asked or told. Students need to know from day 1 what is expected of them and how things are done in the classroom, including how to:

- Enter the classroom

- Settle in their desks

- Put away their lunchboxes and bookbags

- Pay for their lunches

- Sharpen their pencils

- Move around the room

- Line up for lunch

- Go to the bathroom or drinking fountain

- Leave the classroom

- Pass out and pick up papers

- Hand in homework

- Ask a question

- Respond correctly to a question

- Work in groups

- Change groups

- Act when a visitor enters the room

If you want to have an effective classroom, procedures should be established from the opening of school.

First Day Activities

Teachers always want the first day of school to be exciting and special, and so we tend to overplan. Instead, ease into the first day of class, because for your students a school schedule is much more structured than a summer schedule. In the summer, children eat when they want and relax if they are tired. At school, the students eat at lunchtime and after school. Usually by midmorning you will start hearing complaints that their stomach hurts or that they are hungry. This is especially the case with students in kindergarten through second grade. Another complaint is "I'm tired." When you hear this, consider planning a light, healthy snack or playing a game for 10–15 minutes. Diversions help—soon your students will be ready to work once more.

On the first day, it is important to keep activities simple, light, and enjoyable. Plan more than enough activities for the first day, remembering that you will always have tomorrow to finish an activity. Part of being a good teacher is to create a comfortable and relaxed atmosphere for your students. It is also necessary for the teacher to feel calm and comfortable, and being organized and ready for each day will help you feel this way. Relax and enjoy the children. You will not only send home happy children on the first day, but you will also go home with a satisfied and memorable feeling.

On that first day you will have many things to do for yourself and your principal. You will need to teach the procedures and routines that will make your classroom run smoothly. You might want to have an interesting activity sheet and a reading book on students' desks to occupy their time while you are busy obtaining the information you need. Activities could include:

Activity #1: Transportation Arithmetic

Prepare several cutouts of a bicycle, shoe, car, and a bus. Have each child select the cutout that shows the method of transportation they will be using to go home that day. Ask them to color and put their name on the cutout. Next, graph the results on a large piece of paper and have the students make up addition and subtraction math problems using the information on the graph. This is a great way to have math the first day as well as know how your students will be going home.

Activity #2: Birthday Chart

Prepare paper birthday cakes using the school's die-cut machine or purchase them from a school supply store. Have each child put his or her name and birth date on the cutout. Create a graph with the birthday cakes on a large sheet of paper, printing the names of the months of the year at the bottom. Instantly, you learn:

- If the child knows his or her birthday.

- How many birthdays are in each month.

- If you have any children with the same birthdays. (This activity could be used for another math or graphing activity. A permanent birthday chart could be made to hang in the classroom to honor each child as his or her birthday approaches.)

Activity #3: Rule Selection

The first day is also a good time to discuss classroom rules. Place a sticky note on each child's desk. Have them write what they think should be the most important rule for the classroom. Collect the notes and sort them into categories. Group similar suggestions together. After separating the suggestions into categories, you will find that you have your basic class rules. Discuss the suggestions, asking students if they think they can live with these rules. If they agree, these become your classroom rules. Post them in an obvious location for reference.

Activity #4: Student Roles

Have your students write a sentence titled "My Most Important Job as a Student." This could be written on the board as a title or an incomplete topic sentence. Following the format used with the classroom rules, a list of goals for your class could be generated.

Activity #5: Teacher Roles

Have your students write a sentence titled "My Teacher's Most Important Job." Again, this may be written on the board as a title or as an incomplete topic sentence. Use this as the writing of the day.

Activity #6: Pantomiming

For a quick break, have students pantomime favorite activities, such as playing baseball, catching a fish, or throwing a stick for a dog. Start by giving a child a ball to hold during his or her turn. When done, the child throws the ball to the next child, who will then pantomime another favorite activity.

Activity #7: Name Jumble

Mix up letters of a child's name on the chalkboard. The child who guesses correctly gets to mix up the next child's name. This could be done in small groups as a break.

Activity #8: Charades

With older students, have each student or team role-play a favorite sport, hobby, book, and so on. The others watch and try to guess what the activity is. The person or team that guesses correctly will have the opportunity to start next.

Activity #9: Acrostic Poem

Have older children make an acrostic poem with their name and use adjectives that describe themselves. For example, Tim might write:

Thoughtful

Intelligent

Muscular

Activity #10: Name Tag Bulletin Board Game

This getting-acquainted activity is enjoyed by most younger children. First, prior to the beginning of school, prepare a bulletin board with a scene such as a large tree in the background. It should be big enough to display all the name tags and pictures. Next, make a name tag for each child, perhaps in the shape of an apple. Feel free to use your creativity, but be sure the tags will fit on the board you construct.

Activity #10: Setup

1. *Collect Pictures*—Collect both a current and a baby picture of each child. (Be sure each has the child's name on the back.) These photos can be requested in your supply list at the beginning of the year.

2. *Distribute Name Tags*—Have the children wear the name tags until you feel both you and the class know everyone's name. Be sure to prepare a few extra tags in case new students enroll or a tag is lost. Since these name tags can be used for other activities, encourage children to preserve them throughout orientation.

3. *Collect Name Tags*—Once you become familiar with all the children's names, have them remove their name tags.

4. *Affix Tags and Current Pictures to Board*—Take all collected *current* pictures and place them on the board next to each child's name tag.

5. *Identify Baby Picture*—Select a handful of baby pictures each day (for most classes, four is a good number). Put these pictures in a designated area in the front of the room. Now the fun begins. Ask the children if they can identify any of their classmates. Give a small reward to the child who first identifies the pictured child correctly. If the class experiences difficulty identifying the picture, provide clues. For example, say, "He has blond hair and freckles."

6. *Place the Baby Picture Next to the Matching Name Tag*—After the baby picture is identified, place it beside that child's current picture.

Try to give all the children a chance to participate successfully. You might even allow the last child who correctly identified the baby picture to have the opportunity to choose the next participant. As you proceed with this game, the children will get excited and wonder whose picture will be chosen next.

Activity #11: School Supply Drawing

This activity is great for the first day of a new school year because it introduces your students to the supplies you expect them to have for your class.

Activity #11 Setup

1. Prior to the first day of school, purchase one complete set of items each child will need during the school year. (For example, a loose-leaf binder, notebook paper, two pencils, scissors, and a small notepad for homework assignments.) Next, write dual sets of numbers on 3 × 5 cards. For example, the first card has the numeral 1 written on the left side and again on the

right side. Create enough for all your students to have a number, plus a few more for new students. Place the cards in a large box near the entrance of the classroom.

2. As the children come in on the first day, have them draw one set of numbers from the box. As soon as they have picked a number out of the box, have them separate each number, keeping one for themselves and putting the other into a new box. Explain that you will be giving prizes away at the end of the day.

3. Toward the end of the day bring out the school supplies and show them one by one to the class. As each is shown and explained, draw a number from the box. The student with the matching number wins the item. Have enough items, such as pencils, so that each child wins something.

Activity #12: Classroom Bingo Game

This activity is wonderful to use as a first-day getting-acquainted game for intermediate classes. It can be a one- or two-day activity. Allow at least an hour or an hour and a half for part 1 of this activity.

1. Part 1: Line the students up in a large circle according to their birthdays, one month at a time. For example, have all of the January birthday students come up to the front of the room and have them stand in chronological order according to the birthday. Next, repeat with the February birthday students. After all the months have been called, every student should be standing in a large circle. Go around the circle naming each student alternately an "A" or a "B." Then, have them all sit down while still in the circle. Tell them that each of the "A" students is going to interview the "B" student who is seated to the left. Discuss what a good interview should include. Talk about specific questions they might ask each other (e.g., "How many members are in your family?" or "What did you do that was fun this past summer?" or "Which kinds of pets do you have?" or "What is your favorite food?"). Each interview will last 5 minutes. Students should take notes, so they can share what they have learned with the class. After the first round of interviews, the teacher rings a bell to show that the partners need to change roles.

2. Part 2: Ask for volunteer pairs who would be willing to come up to the front of the class to tell what they have learned about their partners. Before they begin, tell your students that they must be very good listeners because later in the day (or even the next day) they will be asked to remember what they have learned.

   While the partners are sharing what they have learned, write down notes on anything unique to each student. If an interview did not disclose anything unique, probe further to discover something about that child. It may take several days for all the pairs to share.

3. Part 3: Provide each student with a blank handout of the Classroom Bingo game sheet (see Form 3.1) and a complete list of the students' names. On the overhead projector, the teacher should display a Classroom Bingo chart that has something unique about each student randomly written in the boxes (this is where your notes from Part 2 are essential). If there are too many boxes, it's fine to use two clues from someone's interview, or you can add clues about yourself or another person with whom the children might be familiar.

Next, the students match the names to each clue. You can do this as a group or by allowing the children to work individually. If done individually, check to see who has the most correct matches. The student with the most matches wins the game. If completed as a group, use your discretion to reward either the entire class or the most active participants.

Although this game requires a substantial bit of time to implement all of the components, it involves many processes that are important to good learning. Listening and communicating, memorization, and note-taking skills are all practiced while students learn about each other.

Activity #13: A Time Capsule about Me

This is a great activity to check writing skills on the first day. Have the students write about themselves (see Form 3.2). They will also draw a picture of themselves. Tell them you are going to place their papers in an enclosed container and that you will save it. At the end of the school year, share it with the students. They always enjoy seeing and comparing their growth.

Activity Recap

These activities are all part of classroom management. The sooner you establish rules and a collaborative environment, the sooner active learning will take place. Students need to know that they have the power to make their classroom a successful learning environment.

After all the opening activities are finished, it is best to start the curriculum, perhaps with the first story in the students' reading book. It is important that the students get into a routine as soon as possible. Students feel secure in a well-structured classroom. To help keep the class focused and the day on track, a copy of the schedule should be posted in the classroom.

Routine Activities for Learning

It is important to have a classroom that elicits creativity and learning. Children wonder what their teacher and classroom will be like long before the first day. Evidence of wonderful activities in a colorful room will excite the students and the parents. Consider some of these ideas when setting up your classroom.

Student of the Week

It is human nature to enjoy recognition for positive behavior. The attention reinforces good behavior and lets the children realize their actions do not go unnoticed. Many teachers like to recognize a student each week. You might have a special bulletin board with some of their work, a picture of the student, and a certificate of some kind.

Some teachers have their students write a note as part of their writing class or morning work explaining why they think this child was chosen. Then the teacher puts the notes on the bulletin

board for all to see. Students do notice when their peers are achieving or improving. It is a lifelong skill and a lesson they need to learn. Thinking about others instead of themselves is an important skill. At the end of the week, the student of the week will be able to take the notes home to share with his or her family. This is a rewarding activity.

Cooperative Learning

At the beginning of the year it is necessary to spend quality time with your students building on the concept of why it is important to be helpful and cooperative with each other. You will be surprised how many children cannot relate well with peers. They either want to work by themselves or with their friends. Students need to learn why it is important to be able to communicate and work with all their peers.

You can teach cooperative learning by providing the class (or smaller teams) with situations for them to resolve through role playing. For example, you might tell them about a bully who won't let others play on the swings or about a child who is too bossy to his or her classmates. Have the students suggest positive ways to settle the situation on their own.

Reading book excerpts aloud and discussing the situation faced by characters can also foster cooperation. Have the children suggest why a given situation occurred and what the characters could have done to make it better.

Many teachers use the strategy of "try three before me." This means the students are expected to try three positive solutions to a conflict before involving the teacher (assuming there is no immediate danger to the situation). Shower students with praise if they manage to do this. You will be pleasantly surprised at the number of children who will try to emulate the behavior.

Using Centers in the Classroom

Centers are areas set aside from the normal teaching area where children can work independently on individual projects or activities. Many of these activities tie into current lessons to reinforce material, such as math manipulatives, science materials, reading, or writing materials.

Since there are both benefits and costs associated with the use of learning centers in the classroom, their use is sometimes controversial. Some advocates believe centers are a necessity and plan 20 minutes a day in their schedule for their use. Other advocates believe centers serve as a learning activity or a reward when students finish their class work. On the other hand, some opponents feel students who do their work properly will not have time for centers. Others believe centers waste valuable instructional time. As the instructor, it is up to you to decide if the use of centers would complement your teaching.

Centers can be educational, challenging, and fun. They need not be a lot of work. The simplest of centers are often the best and can be developed and maintained by a dependable parent. Centers can enhance the units you are studying, be a cumulative review of skills, or be used to introduce something different and challenging.

Your choice of centers will depend on your grade level and the space you have. You may use tables that can hold the materials. If space is an issue, many discount stores offer stackable pullout drawers in which each drawer can be a center.

Once you have set up your centers, practice using the centers. Take a week or longer to introduce one center at a time. Model the way each center works and how to properly use the materials. When it comes to cleanup time, the students should always be responsible for putting the centers back in order or for replacing the drawers.

Suggested ideas for centers include:

1. *Pattern Making*—Place pipe cleaners in a basket with colored beads. Have the students see how many creative patterns they can make. To extend this activity, students can use crayons to complete pattern worksheets, so you could see their favorite patterns (see Form 3.3 at the end of this chapter).

2. *Pattern Blocks*—You can buy pattern-block books, laminate the pages, and challenge your students to find the corresponding blocks.

3. *Writing*—In a basket, place clipboards that contain a plastic overhead transparency with a lined sheet of paper underneath. Give students an erasable pen and let them quietly go to any part of the room to write a story. You can provide story starters if you prefer. Allow a few minutes at some point during the day to put students' stories on the overhead projector to share them with the class.

4. *Gears*—You can buy gear parts through a school supply catalog or store. All students love putting together the gears, so they connect and move. Watching something they have created becomes an exciting adventure in learning.

5. *Art*—Place in a basket some crayons, markers, stencils, scissors with fancy edges, glue sticks, and different sizes of construction paper leftovers. Encourage the students to cut, paste, and design cards for their parents, other school staff members, and friends.

6. *Puzzles*—You can buy small puzzles, which the students can work on at their desks or on the floor. Make sure you mark the back of each puzzle's pieces with a letter or number, so the puzzle pieces will be easy to put back when finished. For example, all pieces of one puzzle might be marked with the letter "A." This is a great help at cleanup time.

7. *Estimation Challenge*—Gather a variety of medication bottles. Fill several bottles with different types of items, such as dried pasta, paper clips, and cotton balls. Challenge the students to record their best guess as to how many objects are

in each container (see Form 3.4). They should write in crayon, so their guess cannot be changed. Then have them count the actual number of items in the bottle and mark the number on the handout. Finally, have them find the difference. How close was their answer? This is a great estimation lesson.

8. *Computer Activities*—Your library might have a variety of reading or math computer games. Many teachers acquire points from student purchases through book clubs and can redeem them for additional software.

9. *Lock Blocks*—These locking plastic shapes can be used to teach geometric figures. You can find them in school supply catalogs and stores.

10. *Tangrams*—A variety of flat, plastic geometric shapes can be used in the study of math or to form animals and other objects. Students can try to replicate patterns found in books of tangrams.

11. *Word Search*—Students walk around the room and find as many words as they can that they know and five words that they want to learn. Students write the words on a clipboard.

12. *Library*—Have select groups of students go to the library at this time. Some teachers assign groups according to rows.

13. *Books on Tape*—This is a great way to have students practice reading along while listening.

14. *Games*—Students love strategy games, such as checkers and Monopoly.

15. *Flash Cards*—Use these for extra practice with math facts.

16. *Sentence Strips or Word Cards*—These can be used in a variety of ways:

   • To alphabetize words

   • To put a story in order

   • To find homophones, antonyms, or synonyms

   • To make a complete sentence

   • To put words into a sentence

17. *Magnets*—Using a magnet and any selection of items you have available, have the children guess which items are magnetic and then check their guesses.

18. *Microscope Study*—Purchase a small, durable microscope and have the children draw the variety of patterns they see when examining small items.

Using Portfolios in Your Classroom

The word *portfolios* can sound a bit intimidating. Though a portfolio sounds like a technically complex and time-consuming task, creating portfolios can be quite rewarding. Most important, portfolios provide a wonderful way to showcase the work of your students.

What Are Portfolios?

A portfolio is simply a collection of several types of completed work and assessments. The purpose is to provide a comprehensive sample of the variety of work performed by the student. It can be as simple as putting each student's work into a file folder, a large manila envelope, booklets, or a plastic box or bin labeled with the student's name. For intermediate students, the work could be collected in a three-ring binder and arranged according to each subject or category.

When first meeting with the parents, inform them they may not see as many papers come home as they might expect. Explain that you are putting most of their child's work into an individual portfolio that will be given to them at the end of the year. However, encourage parents to ask to see their child's portfolio at any time. Be sure to share their child's portfolio with them at each conference.

To develop outstanding portfolios, ask your students what *quality work* is. Students are more likely to follow guidelines they have helped create. Post their ideas on a rubric (guideline) chart, similar to the following example:

Quality Work Includes . . .
1. Name and date
2. Neat handwriting
3. Good punctuation
4. Careful spelling
5. (Any additional items specific to the day's lesson)

Incorporate into each writing lesson a reminder of the rubric and encourage students to look for these standards in their work. When revising or editing, have students work with partners to check to see if they have followed the guidelines. This will ensure that they are on the right track for quality work.

When introducing a new theme or lesson, be sure you have a finished product in mind. Have students date all work to allow you to track their progress throughout the year. Though it might take a while for the students to complete a project, each finished work will build the students' confidence. Save these projects and add them to their portfolios.

By maintaining children's portfolios, you will be well on your way to showcasing your students' work during academic night, an event held by many schools toward the end of the school year. When this night arrives, display all of the portfolios and individual projects for parents, students, and friends to enjoy.

What to Include in Portfolios

Portfolios should include a good cross-section of papers, projects, and assessments. Start collecting the samples early in the year, so you can illustrate the improvement the child has made.

You may wish to include a reading list with the titles of each book the child has read throughout the year. (It may be easier for each student to track this for you. See Form 3.5.) Ideally, every student will have several pages of this list by the end of the year. You may be surprised to learn how many books your class has read throughout the year! You might even choose to give an award or certificate for the year's most avid reader!

Additional suggested items for portfolios include:

Reading

- Reading assessments

- Vocabulary and other reading worksheets

- Group projects

- Reading inventories

- Surveys of reading interests

- Special story maps and time lines

- Various comprehension skill sheets covering topics such as main idea, sequencing, context clues, and so on

Writing

- Simple completed stories

- Activity sheets that have edited sentences

- Expository writing, such as giving directions, writing to persuade, giving opinions, and writing to inform

- Worksheets that illustrate writing strategies, such as being focused, using transition words, using good leads and endings, and providing ample details

- Graphic organizers

- Examples of topic sentences and essay conclusions

- Language or grammar activities or worksheets

- Handwriting samples

Science and Social Studies

- Diagrams

- Quizzes and other assessments

- Experiments

- Samples of class work from each chapter in the textbooks

- Reports

· Vocabulary activity sheets

· Projects

Math

· Word problems

· Number sense activities

· Math fact quiz sheets

· Activities involving fractions, geometrical designs or problems, money, time, fractions, and so on

Making Portfolios Work for You

Portfolios will work for you if you have a good system in place for keeping them neat and orderly. Start out the year explaining to your students that you expect them to be in charge of their own portfolios. Take the time to train your students on how to put their work into their portfolios. Never allow them to keep the portfolios in their desks. Collect the portfolios daily and put them in a special place in the classroom, such as a shelf, a table, or a plastic bin specially designed to hold hanging files or binders. Have a special time set aside each week when students add new items to their portfolios. Be specific as to where you want each item to be placed in the portfolios. Consider having a buddy system, where pairs of students help each other make sure that they organize their work properly. Alternatively, appoint capable student assistants to help you file papers in the portfolios.

Using Your Portfolios

There are many great uses for portfolios. One of the more important uses is to share them with parents during conferences. By saving a cross-section of papers in portfolios, parents can easily see the progression of instruction for the grading period or semester. This helps parents acquire a positive attitude toward their child's teacher and the education their child is receiving.

Portfolios also serve as documentation for student progress. If a child is not making the expected progress, the portfolio's contents will illustrate this.

The portfolios can also be helpful when doing report cards. You will have samples of each student's work in front of you, allowing you to see the progress made or needs for improvement. Portfolios also can be a resource for writing comments on report cards.

Once you have a comfortable system in place, you will feel more at ease using student portfolios. Start small and expand their use each year. You will be surprised how you add to and improve your portfolio system with each passing year. Your students and their parents will be grateful for your efforts.

Preparing for Open House

The first Open House for new teachers can be a daunting experience. However, if you plan to do some of the following items, you will probably have a very pleasant experience.

Inviting Your Parents

The most important goal is to get the parents to attend the Open House. If you talk in advance about the Open House with your students, chances are they will ask their parents to come. Have the students write an invitation to their parents. The message should convey how much they want their parents to attend. Invite parents early and send reminders.

Greeting Your Parents

Your first concern may be "Will they like me?" This is a normal concern because we all have a desire to be liked. However, remember the parents also will want to make a positive impression. It is important to come across as a friendly and positive person. Have name tags on your students' desks, and ask the parents, if possible, to sit at their child's desk. By doing this, you can easily associate the child with the parent. This will help you remember the parents.

Make it a habit to greet the parents in a sincere fashion, using good eye contact when you welcome them. This will give your parents the message that they are important to you and you are glad they came.

Make the room look inviting. After all, your parents are leaving their child in your care for a good part of the day. It is important for them to know that their child will be happy in this new learning environment. If you have a hall outside your door, have the students decorate it with a welcome theme for their parents. You could have them create a welcome banner, special art work, or short stories accompanied by a drawing about their family. This gives the parents something engaging to read.

When the parents enter your classroom, have a sign-in table for them (see Form 3.6). Also provide a volunteer sign-up sheet on a table for those who might wish to help you. Have the sheet organized into categories so that you can see how they are willing to help. (See Volunteer Sign-up Sheet, Form 3.7 at the end of this chapter.) You might ask which day is best suited for them, what time, and how often they would like to work. Leave a section for moms who would like to do things at home but are unable to come to school. You might even have another sheet for parents who would like to drive on field trips or help furnish treats and assist with school parties.

Activities for Parents

After the parents are seated, invite them to do a few activities. One suggestion would be to have a letter from their child, a 2×2 sticky note and a cutout heart on top of each desk. The children's letters should reflect how happy they are that their parents are present. They might also tell a little about what they want their parents to see, such as their clean desk with all their new books inside.

The sticky note is for the parents. Have them write what they feel *their* most important goal is for their child's education. Ask them to place their note on a large cutout heart in the front of the room reserved for that purpose. Later, the parents can read the notes and observe what other parents wrote. The next day you can share all their ideas with your students. These ideas will show how the teacher, parent, and student should work together so that learning will be successful.

The cutout heart on each desk is for a personal note from the parents to their child. The child will be thrilled to see the note first thing the next day. Many children keep these endearing notes for a long time in their desks.

Activities for Students

In preparing for Open House purchase ready-made apple cutouts that are about 3 × 5 inches in size. Have them laminated, so they will stay strong. About a week before Open House, have the students practice writing a "Dear Mom and Dad" message to their parents. For example:

Dear Mom and Dad,

Thank you for always being there for me.

> *Love,*
> *Brian*

After they have polished their note, they then use a permanent marker to write their message on the apple. (If a child makes a mistake, use nail polish remover to erase.) When the notes are complete, put a magnetic strip on the back of each apple. On the night of Open House, put a small piece of masking tape on the back of each apple and place them all in the form of a heart on your classroom door or chalkboard. At the end of Open House, tell the parents that their children each made a special magnet that can be used to hold their spelling word lists on the refrigerator. Have the parents take their magnets home.

Handouts for Your Parents

Include informational handouts on each desk, such as your classroom schedule, supply list, wish list, and information about the curriculum. Encourage parents to use the schedule to plan visits, such as occasional lunches with their child. The supply list is helpful to have so parents ensure their child has the needed supplies. A wish list encourages parents to contribute to the classroom. Some ideas for this list are tissues, liquid soap, egg cartons, magnetic tape, markers, pipe cleaners, cotton balls, sequins, yarn, and so on.

Another suggestion is to make a drawing of a big tree on a chalkboard or on a large piece of paper. Cut out an equal number of red and white apples on the die-cut machine. On top of the red apple, name a classroom item on your wish list. On the bottom of the white apple, name the item again and add a space marked NAME _____. Staple the red apple on top of the white apple at the top. Place them on the tree. The parent who wishes to buy that item tears off the top red apple to keep and writes their name on the bottom white apple. That allows the teacher to know which parent will provide the item. Alternatively, give this list to your parents at the beginning of the year:

- Napkins

- Paper plates

- White paper bags (good for Valentines' bags)

- Paper cups

- Potting soil

- Glue sticks (nonliquid kind)

- Crayons and markers (both broad and fine tip)

- Pizza pie cardboard circles (great for games and fractions)

- Wallpaper books

- Travel brochures

- Yarn in several colors

- Glitter/Sequins

- Magnetized sticky strips

- Sticky tack notes

- Microphone and speakers (a karaoke machine is wonderful)

- Egg cartons

- Nerf ball

- Small clock faces for individual use

- Math facts card sets

- Playing cards

- Liquid soap

- Learning board games

- Trifold project display boards

- Tissues

- First-aid kit

- Name tags for field trips

Most parents are excited about starting the year off right and want to help their child's class. This gives them the opportunity to contribute.

Items to Discuss with Parents

Every parent will want to know about curriculum and what their child will be doing in each subject. Open House is the perfect opportunity to briefly discuss these things. The following is a list of items you might want to include:

- Introduction about yourself

- Attendance/Tardy policy

- Grading system (how you grade and what you grade)

- Conference expectations

- Homework policy

- Discipline policy/classroom rules

- Birthday celebrations (optional)

- Curriculum

- State standards and standardized tests

- Daily schedule

- Goals (classroom and individual)

- Lunchroom policies

- Recreational reading recommendations

- Book reports

One-Hundred Day Activities

Plan a special day for the 100th day of school. It's a nice time to revel in the fact that the students have been in school for more than half of the school year. Make it an exciting day using the skills the students have already learned. Consider doing one or more of the following:

1. Write 100 words.

2. Find 100 words that begin with the letter ____.

3. Do a place value activity with any number over 100, for example, 124. Using beans or any other small items, glue 100 beans to one paper, 20 to another, and finally 4 to the last. Label the ones, tens, and hundreds correctly.

4. String 100 pieces of Fruit Loops cereal to a string and place the strings in outside trees for the birds to eat.

5. Measure items around the room that are about 100 centimeters long.

6. Count to 100 by ones, twos, threes, fours, and so on. Try counting backwards from 100 to 1. (See Forms 3.8–3.14 for this activity at the end of the chapter.)

7. Make a picture with 100 cotton balls.

8. Make 100 Valentines for a nursing home.

9. Write a story about the 100th day using 100 words.

10. Measure your height with a string. Beside the string lay out 1-inch square manipulatives. Find everyone's height in square inches. Is it less than or greater than 100? Write a number sentence to tell the answer.

11. Sit and do nothing for 100 seconds. Then write your name as many times as possible for 100 seconds. Discuss which seemed to take the longer time.

12. Lightly bounce in place for 100 seconds, counting aloud. Record how many times everyone jumped. After resting, try the activity again. Try to increase the number of jumps.

13. List as many places as you can that you'd like to visit. Name a few. Why do you want to go to those places? Discuss. Can the class list 100 collectively?

14. As another place value activity, hand each student a piece of plain paper. Tell the students that you are only going to give them 100 seconds to complete this activity. Have them write X as many times as they can in 100 seconds. When you have called time, have each student go back and circle every group of ten X's on their paper. Have them write the following sentences: I have _____ groups of 10 and _____ ones remaining. My number is _____.

Form 3.1

Classroom Bingo

B	I	N	G	O
1				
2				
3				
4				
5				
6				

Form 3.2

A Time Capsule about Me

Write in your answers now. Then we'll save our time capsule. In the spring, we will read it again and see how we've grown.

1. Date _____.

2. My whole name is _____.

3. My favorite food is _____.

4. My favorite color is _____.

5. My best friend's name is _____.

6. My favorite song is _____.

7. My favorite game is _____.

8. The thing I like to do most is _____.

9. My favorite sport is _____.

10. My favorite TV show is _____.

11. When I grow up, I want to be a _____.

12. My favorite book is _____.

13. My favorite subject is _____.

14. Something you should know about me is _____.

Draw a picture of how you look now on the back of this page. What color are your eyes, your hair, and your clothes? Label your picture "My first day of school."

Form 3.3

Pattern Activity

Name: _____   Date: _____

Directions: Using a pipe cleaner and colored beads, try to make as many patterns as possible. Color each pattern that you make on the following lines.

1. OOOOOOOOOOOOOOOOOOOO

2. OOOOOOOOOOOOOOOOOOOO

3. OOOOOOOOOOOOOOOOOOOO

4. OOOOOOOOOOOOOOOOOOOO

5. OOOOOOOOOOOOOOOOOOOO

6. OOOOOOOOOOOOOOOOOOOO

7. OOOOOOOOOOOOOOOOOOOO

8. OOOOOOOOOOOOOOOOOOOO

9. OOOOOOOOOOOOOOOOOOOO

10. OOOOOOOOOOOOOOOOOOOO

In the space below, tell which pattern was your favorite and why.

Form 3.4

Estimation Challenge

Name: _____   Date: _____

Directions: Look at each numbered bottle. Write down how many you *think* is in each bottle (use a red crayon to record your guess). Then, count the items. Put the amount you counted on the second line (in blue crayon). How close was your guess? Can you figure it out?

Bottle #	Best Guess	Actual Count	Difference
#1	_____	_____	_____
#2	_____	_____	_____
#3	_____	_____	_____
#4	_____	_____	_____
#5	_____	_____	_____
#6	_____	_____	_____
#7	_____	_____	_____
#8	_____	_____	_____

Form 3.5

Books I Have Read

Student's Name _____

Grade Level _____

_____ Title of Book _____

Main Characters _____

_____

_____

This story is about _____

_____

_____

_____

I (liked/did not like) this story because _____

_____

_____

_____ Title of Book _____

Main Characters _____

_____

_____

This story is about _____

_____

_____

_____

I (liked/did not like) this story because _____

_____

_____

Form 3.6

Open House Attendance

Parents:

    Please sign below and indicate your child's name. Your child will be proud to see that you attended our meeting!

    Thank you for coming tonight!

Parent's or Guardian's Name(s)	Child's Name
1.	
2.	
3.	
4.	
5.	
6.	
7.	
8.	
9.	
10.	
11.	
12.	
13.	
14.	
15.	
16.	
17.	
18.	
19.	
20.	
21.	
22.	
23.	
24.	
25.	

Form 3.7

Volunteer Sign-up Sheet

Dear Parents,

    Volunteers are an integral part of our education curriculum. With your invaluable help, we can meet the needs of our students much more efficiently.

    If you feel that you would like to volunteer, even if you cannot come to school, I would greatly appreciate and welcome your help. As you can see by the categories listed, there are many ways in which your services can be used.

    Please indicate which category interests you most. Include your phone number and the day(s) and time(s) you would be available. Indicate in the comments section if you prefer to help from your home, such as preparing treats, making bulletin board items, and so on.

    Thank you for all your help!

Sincerely,

Volunteer Categories

Classroom: _____ Mentor _____ At home volunteer _____ Tutor

Events: _____ Chaperone _____ Parties _____ Assistant
for field trips

Volunteer Name: _____ Phone: _____

Days you're available: _____ Times: _____

Additional Comments:

Form 3.8

Let's Count to 100: Count by _Ones_:

1 _____ _____ _____ _____ _____ _____ _____ _____ _____ _____

_____ _____ _____ _____ _____ _____ _____ _____ _____ _____

_____ _____ _____ _____ _____ _____ _____ _____ _____ _____

_____ _____ _____ _____ _____ _____ _____ _____ _____ _____

_____ _____ _____ _____ _____ _____ _____ _____ _____ _____

_____ _____ _____ _____ _____ _____ _____ _____ _____ _____

_____ _____ _____ _____ _____ _____ _____ _____ _____ _____

_____ _____ _____ _____ _____ _____ _____ _____ _____ _____

_____ _____ _____ _____ _____ _____ _____ _____ _____ _____

_____ _____ _____ _____ _____ _____ _____ _____ _____ _____

Form 3.9

Count by _Twos_ to 100:

2	_____	_____	_____	_____
_____	_____	_____	_____	_____
_____	_____	_____	_____	_____
_____	_____	_____	_____	_____
_____	_____	_____	_____	_____
_____	_____	_____	_____	_____
_____	_____	_____	_____	_____
_____	_____	_____	_____	_____
_____	_____	_____	_____	_____
_____	_____	_____	_____	_____

**Draw two groups of two pigs playing in the mud:**

Form 3.10

Count by _Threes_ to 100:

<u>__3__</u>   <u>_____</u>   <u>_____</u>   <u>_____</u>   <u>_____</u>

<u>_____</u>   <u>_____</u>   <u>_____</u>   <u>_____</u>   <u>_____</u>

<u>_____</u>   <u>_____</u>   <u>_____</u>   <u>_____</u>   <u>_____</u>

<u>_____</u>   <u>_____</u>   <u>_____</u>   <u>_____</u>   <u>_____</u>

<u>_____</u>   <u>_____</u>   <u>_____</u>   <u>_____</u>   <u>_____</u>

<u>_____</u>   <u>_____</u>   <u>_____</u>   <u>_____</u>   <u>_____</u>

<u>_____</u>   <u>_____</u>   <u>__99__</u>

**Draw three groups of three ships in the sea:**

Form 3.11

Count by _Fours_ to 100:

4 _____   _____   _____   _____   _____

_____   _____   _____   _____   _____

_____   _____   _____   _____   _____

_____   _____   _____   _____   _____

_____   _____   _____   _____   _____

Draw four groups of four birds sitting in a tree:

Form 3.12

Count by _Fives_ to 100:

5			
			100

Draw and color five groups of five flowers in a beautiful garden:

Form 3.13

Count by _Tens_ to 100:

__10__   _____   _____   _____   _____

_____   _____   _____   _____   _____

**Draw ten groups of ten red hearts and circle them:**

Form 3.14

Let's Count From 100 to 1—_Backwards!_

100 ____ ____ ____ ____ ____ ____ ____ ____ ____

____ ____ ____ ____ ____ ____ ____ ____ ____

____ ____ ____ ____ ____ ____ ____ ____ ____

____ ____ ____ ____ ____ ____ ____ ____ ____

____ ____ ____ ____ ____ ____ ____ ____ ____

____ ____ ____ ____ ____ ____ ____ ____ ____

____ ____ ____ ____ ____ ____ ____ ____ ____

____ ____ ____ ____ ____ ____ ____ ____ ____

____ ____ ____ ____ ____ ____ ____ ____ **1**

**Draw and color ten groups of ten chocolate chip cookies on blue plates:**

4

Planning and Scheduling

Scheduling Classes to Work for You

Scheduling can at times be a real challenge for new and experienced teachers. Covering an expansive curriculum in a short period of time requires a creative teacher and a flexible schedule. It's important that you find a schedule that works for you and yet is flexible enough so that unforeseen interruptions don't cause chaos.

A Five-Day Schedule

If you are on a regular five-day schedule, with special area classes on the same day each week, then it will be up to you to plug in the correct number of minutes for each subject required each day. The curriculum guideline you receive each year tells you what you are to teach and how many minutes per week you need for each subject. You then decide how to schedule these minutes in your day. Some subjects, such as math, reading, and writing, need to be taught each day, while others could be spaced in intervals throughout the week.

On days in which you have special areas, such as art and music, or special events, try to combine several subject areas. For example, if you invite a guest speaker to speak on bats, you might read aloud a book about bats and talk about their environment. You can then include a writing lesson with this information. Doing this allows you to incorporate a reading lesson with writing, social studies, and science, which leaves time for a math lesson. Your requirements have been filled, and the day was a success without a lot of extra stress.

You can also coordinate with the art and music teacher concerning special themes in your classroom. For example, if you are studying about the Native American Sioux, you might read aloud about where and how they live and about their culture. Then, when the students go to art class, they can do a project with pictographs or Native American motifs. In music, students might learn the beat of ancient drum songs. When teachers work together, students remember better because they can tie important ideas from different classes together. Instead of having a fragmented day, students enjoy a cohesive learning experience. Children love these days because they are interactive, entertaining, focused, and educational.

The way you plan and coordinate your schedule and curriculum is key to an effective lesson. In response to busy schedules and demands on curriculum, creative teachers incorporate several subjects into a lesson with better results. Also, by coordinating all areas of the curriculum, you encourage quality projects, writing, and artwork, which can then be displayed and shared with parents when they visit their child's classroom.

A Six-Day Schedule

Many schools are resorting to six-day schedules, with specialists (music and art teachers) rotating among schools. This schedule can be difficult because you have to think of your days as day 1, day 2, day 3, and so on, up to day 6, instead of Monday, Tuesday, Wednesday, Thursday, and Friday. Some schools try to schedule art or music back-to-back with physical education, so the teacher has a longer planning period. This is very helpful if it can be done.

When planning a six-day schedule, it is helpful to sit down and plan for three different master schedules. One schedule would be for music day, another for art day, and the other for a normal school day. Plug in the time you have the special classes and your regular planning time, then work the curriculum around it, using creative lessons like those described earlier.

When you have your art, music, and regular schedules determined and typed, copy each of the three schedules on different colored paper and laminate them. Use the laminated schedules as part of your substitute teacher's packet, so the substitute can be informed when you are not in class. You can then include lesson details, such as story titles and subject areas, for the substitute's lesson plan. Turn in a copy of the schedule to the office, so they know where your class is at all times (see Form 4.1 as an example). Also put a copy in your lesson plan book.

One great idea is to put your teachers' manuals on your desk with a bookmark to indicate your current lesson. Put the master lesson plans on top before leaving school. Should an emergency occur, you are prepared.

The following is an example of a six-day plan.

Master Schedule Example for Day 1 (Music offered today)

8:40–8:50 Homeroom Time—Children come in and do the flow-chart activities on the chalkboard and overhead projector. A brief language activity is written on the chalkboard. A Problem of the Day in math is displayed on the overhead projector. Students need to be reminded at this time to make sure they have gone to the bathroom, had their drinks, and sharpened their pencils for the day. Do not allow anyone to sharpen pencils after the bell or have a bathroom break until 10:00 a.m., unless it is an emergency.

8:50–9:00 Announcements, National Anthem, and Pledge—These will be on television or the intercom.

9:00–9:30 Administrative Tasks—Students finish their language activity and daily math problem while you take attendance and the lunch count. When you are finished, tell the students to take out a marker and put their pencils away. They will correct their morning work. If they are not finished, they must finish in marker; this tells you who is working.

9:30–10:30 Writer's Workshop—Start with a minilesson to use in students' writing. This usually takes 10–15 minutes.

Writing Time: Review the rules for writing time, which are posted on a chart in the room. The students take out their writing books and work on their own stories. Encourage them to use the minilesson skill in their writing or check for that skill in their work. As they write, walk around the room and encourage the students who have writer's block by having them read their story to you or tell you what they are going to write about. You might be able to give them ideas to help them get started. Writing time usually lasts 20–25 minutes.

Bathroom Break: Walk the children to the bathroom for a 5-minute break. Line leaders are also bathroom monitors. Have students go in four or five at a time. (No talking should occur in the bathroom, or they will get a check on the chalkboard by their name. This is part of the behavior plan.)

Share Time: After returning to the room, pick five or six students to share their writing. The students sit in a semicircle on the floor in front of the room. The student reading sits in a chair. As they listen students should note something they liked or would like to hear more about in the story.

10:30–10:50 Math—See the lesson for the day in the teacher's manual.

10:50–11:30 Music—The music teacher will come into the classroom to teach.

11:30–12:02 Lunch Break—Tell students to bring their money or lunches with them. Make sure the door is closed when you exit the room, and ask line leaders to lead the way.

12:02–12:08 Bathroom Break

12:08–12:30 Math—Finish math lesson.

12:30–1:20 Language Arts—See teacher's manual and lessons prepared on desk.

1:20–1:45 Centers and Small-Group Instruction—Students check the center chart to find which center they are assigned to. One of the centers will be small-group instruction. Work at the reading table in the back of the room using the books marked with the students' names.

1:45–1:50 Clean-up Time—Students straighten the room and prepare for P.E. Have students line up quietly for P.E. The teacher will pick them up at the room and return them at 2:20.

1:50–2:20 Planning Time

2:20–2:40 Science or Social Studies—See plans on desk.

2:40–2:45 Afternoon Announcements—Remind students to be very quiet and listen.

2:45 First Bell–All students who ride buses or who need to pick up a kindergarten sibling are excused.

2:50 Second Bell—All students are dismissed.

2:50–3:15 Preparation Time—Straighten up room, erase the chalkboard, and get the room ready for the next day.

Master Schedule Example for Day 2 (Art class included on this day)

8:40–8:50 Homeroom Time

8:50–9:00 Announcements, National Anthem, and Pledge

9:00–9:30 Administrative Tasks—Students finish their language activity and daily math problem while you take attendance and the lunch count.

9:30–10:30 Writer's Workshop

Writing Time: Allow 20–25 minutes.

Bathroom Break: Allow 5 minutes.

Share Time

10:30–11:30 Math

11:32–12:02 Lunch Break

12:02–12:08 Bathroom Break

12:08–12:48 Language Arts

12:50–1:40 Art Class

1:45–1:50 Clean-up Time—Have students line up quietly for P.E.

1:50–2:20 Planning Time

2:20–2:40 Science or Social Studies

2:40–2:45 Afternoon Announcements

2:45 First Bell—All students who ride buses or who need to pick up a kindergarten sibling are excused.

2:50 Second Bell—All students are dismissed.

2:50–3:15 Preparation Time

Master Schedule Example for Days 3, 4, 5, and 6 (Normal schedule)

8:40–8:50 Homeroom Time

8:50–9:00 Announcements, National Anthem, and Pledge

9:00–9:30 Administrative Tasks

9:30–10:35 Writer's Workshop

Writing Time

Bathroom Break

Share Time

10:35–11:30 Math

11:32–12:02 Lunch Break

12:02–12:08 Bathroom Break

12:08–12:55 Language Arts

12:55–1:20 Science or Social Studies

1:20–1:45 Centers and Small-Group Instruction

1:45–1:50 Clean-up Time—Students straighten the room and prepare for P.E.

1:50–2:20 Planning Time

2:20–2:40 Science or Social Studies

2:40–2:45 Afternoon Announcements

2:45 First Bell—All students who ride buses or who need to pick up a kindergarten sibling should be excused.

2:50 Second Bell—All students are dismissed.

2:50–3:15 Preparation Time

Daily and Weekly Lesson Plans

Teachers who keep daily or weekly lesson plans cover the curriculum better. With tight schedules and constant interruptions, it is especially important to have plans, so you can be sure all the subject areas are taught. It's nice to know that at the end of the week all that was planned was completed.

A lesson plan is your plan of attack to help you best meet the needs of your students. It doesn't have to be elaborate—just user-friendly and functional. Many teachers like using a regular plan book with a square for each subject and day. If you are computer literate, you can write your lesson plans on your schedule. Using a computer allows you to keep plans from year to year. This helps you in planning ahead in your curriculum. Whichever way you choose, it is important to make sure you have a plan and that you use it.

It is wise to jot down notes about your day in your plans. If anything happened that was unusual— a speaker's changed schedule, disciplinary action, and so on—make note in your plans. If you get into a habit of doing this, you might be surprised how often you refer to those notes, especially if a problem arises. Your notes need not be long, just enough to jog your memory.

Most schools collect teachers' lesson plan books at the end of the year as part of their school audit. Sometimes your principal will check to see what you have planned for each week. They have a right to do this, so be prepared and ready.

Planning with Your Team

Finding time to do all the important tasks a teacher must do is difficult, to say the least. However, if you establish a working relationship with your team, you will be surprised by how efficiently your time is spent. Young teachers are eager to do a good job but need input on how to get started and are often worried about if they are doing it right. Working as a team helps guide and teach new teachers what is expected of them so that they can do their best. Sharing worksheet ideas, class projects, and bulletin board ideas are some of the ways a teacher can save time and be more efficient. Remember your primary goal is to make learning come alive in a loving and exciting classroom atmosphere, and working with a team helps you meet that goal.

Teachers who work independently and do not wish to their share ideas stifle their team, which is why everyone on the team should be assigned and contribute to each project so that everyone has input. The last thing you want is to work on a team that is dictated to by one person. In some teams, one teacher leads the group, and the other teachers will say, "Anything is fine with me; just tell me what to do." These teachers are allowing the leader to do the creative work and are not contributing to the team.

Team meetings are vital. Select a time before or after school to meet. Everyone on the team should agree on the time. Make sure your teammates know well in advance, so they will not schedule a conference or another meeting at that time. If possible, take a calendar and mark off dates for the month ahead of time. That way, everyone will be well informed. Some grade-level teams bring their ideas for future units or projects. Together, they decide what they will or will not use. Doing this allows the team to have units or projects ready in advance.

Other teams decide at the beginning of the year which units each teacher will be responsible for developing. This usually works well with teaching teams that have been together for awhile. However, if one of the teachers on the team is new to teaching, it's advisable to work together on units the first year. This helps the new teacher develop his or her own style while contributing ideas to the curriculum. It is important that everyone contributes to and feels a part of the team.

If your team works well together, you can also have your classes work together on projects. Students like doing things together and enjoy being in a new classroom setting. If your entire team does not want to work together, try to find one team member who seems friendly and approach that person with your ideas. Chances are the teacher will be thrilled and delighted to work with you.

Working together makes teaching more fun and less laborious. It helps you understand how to do what is expected of you as a classroom teacher. First-year teachers have a lot of questions, and it is nice to know that there is someone to help you find the answers. Take advantage of the wealth of knowledge that experienced teachers have acquired over the years. Most of them will be very happy to share their ideas and materials with you.

If you can foster a cooperative relationship with your team and work together to plan your curriculum, you will have more time for other teaching responsibilities. Today's curriculum is very demanding, and teachers must learn to be efficient with their time. Establishing a cooperative relationship with your team encourages you keep striving to do your best.

Flexibility

Flexibility is probably the most important word when it comes to teaching. With twenty-five or more students in a classroom, you have to have special tricks up your sleeve at all times. Consider the following example: You are having a great morning, and things are going smoothly. Then there is a fire drill! Your students leave the building in an orderly fashion and go through all the motions. However, after the drill, the students are restless and inattentive. You had several items you wanted to complete, and now you are faced with getting the students calm and back on track. What can you do?

When this happens, one quick way to have your students refocus is to have a brief, quiet teacher read-aloud. Keep on a shelf a selected group of short books on areas of study. Pull one of them at this time and begin reading. Reading helps calm students and allows them to refocus. After reading, proceed to what you were doing before the drill.

You will experience lots of interruptions during the school year, so you need to be prepared for anything. The best teacher is a flexible one who can be interrupted without becoming frustrated. Each class is different. Having some ideas on how to refocus your students' attention is necessary and vital.

The Teachable Moment

Sometimes your class will become sidetracked. You may be teaching a subject and a student asks a question or an explanation is needed. This may be something that has occurred before, and now it needs to be addressed. It may be something that needs explaining before going on with instruction. When this happens, you need to stop and teach about the idea. These occurrences are called teachable moments. Teachable moments might get you off your lesson temporarily, but the investment of this time can be critical to your students' understanding of the material. Many times these unplanned moments can be far better than any planned lesson.

Substitute Teacher Plans

Planning for a substitute is unique to the teaching profession and very important. In almost every other job when an employee is absent, the work just stacks up and waits for the employee's return. In some cases, when the employee is out for an extended period of time, the company hires a temporary person to do the job, but this person does not need plans to do the job. When a teacher is absent, students are still there, waiting to learn, and the schedule must continue as smoothly as possible, or it will be difficult for both the substitute and the classroom teacher. Students seem to sense when a substitute is proficient at his or her job. If they feel the substitute is ill prepared, they will take advantage of the situation and try to get away with inappropriate behavior. It is your job to help your substitute be as prepared as possible in any situation.

At the beginning of the year, make a Substitute Survival Kit. This kit can be in a small, plastic storage box, a large pocket file folder, or a three-ring binder. The kit should be clearly labeled and placed on or near your desktop, where a substitute can easily find it. In case of emergency, or if you're teaching a subject that a substitute might have difficulty following, this Substitute Survival Kit will be of great help. The Substitute Survival Kit includes the following items:

- *Map of School*—A map of the school indicating the location of all school facilities is very important to the substitute teacher. If an inclusive map is prohibitive, be sure to detail key locations, such as P.E. facilities, the cafeteria, the teacher's lounge, and so on.

- *School Directory*—A list of all school personnel is helpful and is something your school almost certainly provides for you. Be sure to note a few teachers (or administrators) who may be of assistance to the substitute, along with their location in the building.

- *Daily Schedule*—Provide a separate schedule for each day of the week. In this way, your substitute will know at a glance what happens on a particular day. The individual daily schedules should be laminated and placed in a three-ring binder so that it is easy to flip from one day to the next. You may also want to have a regular weekly schedule available.

- *Seating Charts*—Since elementary students quite often change their seats for one reason or another, you might find that a simple hand or computer drawing of the students' desks is more functional for you. You can either place the students' names on small sticky notes and move them as needed, or you can write their names in erasable pen on a laminated seating chart.

- *Special Education Schedules*—Be sure to include the schedules of the special education students who go to resource classes. Either incorporate this information into your individual daily schedule or make a separate schedule denoting the day and time the students leave the classroom and where they go (see Form 4.2). Be sure to indicate whether the students are picked up or if they are expected to go by themselves to their other class.

This special schedule should include the following classes:

Classes for specific learning disability (SLD) students

Speech and language classes

English for speakers of other languages (ESOL) classes

Gifted classes

Special reading classes, such as Literacy Success or Reading Recovery

Tutoring programs

Special music or instrumental classes

Also include information about students who go to the clinic for special health problems or medications that need to be administered.

- *Discipline Program*—Provide a brief outline of your discipline program. Make sure it's simple enough for the substitute to easily follow. Some substitute teachers prefer to follow their own plan, which is fine as long as you provide a basis to help the teacher operate the class efficiently.

- *Special Helper List*—Include a list of consistently helpful students. The substitute usually will have questions to ask, and it's nice to have some students who can be trusted to help. Conversely, you may want to provide notice of those students who may provide a challenge. The more the teacher is forewarned regarding individual personalities, the better he or she will be to adapt to the unfamiliar class.

- *Emergency Procedures*—Each school has a unique set of emergency procedures to follow. Most schools document these procedures, and this document can be transferred to the substitute kit. If the information provided is unclear or incomplete, it is important to provide a brief description of each type of emergency along with detailed instructions on procedures to follow. For example, you might note, "Two short blasts from the emergency warning system indicates a tornado warning." Once identified, the teacher can follow the procedures set for the type of emergency, such as moving the children into a basement or windowless hallway.

- *Additional Class Plans*—In case your return is delayed, it is always a good idea to include supplemental worksheets (along with answer keys). The substitute should know where to locate your manuals and long-term class plans to ensure your class does not fall behind in your extended absence.

- *Lunch Procedures*—Though you have already included a class schedule and location of all critical facilities (including the cafeteria or lunch area), you should also include a copy of the procedures for dropping off and retrieving students at lunch.

• *Treats*—As a bonus, you may want to provide the substitute with some rewards for the students. This could be a bag of candy treats (check with the school's policy concerning candy), special passes for homework, extra computer time, special helper assignments, treasure chest items, or bonus stickers.

• *Overview Instructions*—As part of any plan, it is good to have a brief summary of expectations. These should include important times, such as the time a substitute is expected to arrive at a school and any important items particular to your environment. (See Forms 4.3 and 4.4.) Encourage the teacher to have students help in the classroom. For example, the teacher may have the class clean up at the end of the day. You'd be surprised how nice it is to return to a clean classroom.

Being a good substitute is a job in itself. One has to be versatile and ready for any situation. Substitutes may bring favorite games, books, music, songs, or CDs to share with the class. It is also a good idea for substitutes to take time to share a little about themselves, their hobbies, their families or pets, and their likes and dislikes. Children like to be able to identify with a new person. Substitutes also need to be firm but also child-friendly. The classroom is not a place for anyone who does not understand or care for children.

This kit will certainly help the substitute have a successful day, and most likely the substitute will be asked to return to this school when another teacher is absent. It will also help the classroom teacher feel at ease knowing that he or she did the best job possible to plan for a day away from the classroom.

Planning for a Field Trip

Field trips enrich classroom learning and are an exciting way for your students to learn new information. Field trips also require a certain amount of preplanning and foresight on the classroom teacher's part.

Most important, field trips that you plan for your class should be related to your curriculum in a meaningful way. For example, teaching the history of your state or community could be enhanced tremendously by taking a field trip to either a county park or a museum that has artifacts or scenes that depict earlier times in your area. Many plays or musicals can supplement your literature program. Some school districts even have a published list of approved field trip sites. If you are on your own in selecting field trips, think about the places that would make learning come alive for your students. There are zoos, farms, stores, factories, police stations, city government buildings, museums, parks, public libraries, historical societies and buildings, and many other places you could choose from.

There are also "in-house" field trips, which take place when people from your community come to class to share something special with your students. Consider inviting these people to come to your school to give a talk, show a film, or put on a special program. In some instances, in-house field trips are easier than taking the entire class on a trip. Be sure to talk with the person in charge of the outside performers to be sure they know exactly what you are teaching and what you would like them to stress when giving the presentation to your class.

There are many people working in the community who would be happy to come to your class, including nurses, hospital workers, dentists and dental hygienists, gardeners, scientists, authors, government officials, police and paramedics, people who have traveled to various places, volunteers from various organizations, museum and park employees, and others. Using speakers helps you enrich your curriculum and give your students another point of view.

When you decide to take your students on a field trip away from school, it is most important that you plan for every detail. Being completely organized when the children are excited is difficult, so recruit some parents or other volunteers to help you.

Here is a list of some of the things that you must remember to do:

1. As soon as you decide where you would like to take your students, get your principal's input and approval.

2. Write a letter to inform parents/guardians about your upcoming field trip. Give them the details of the trip far enough in advance to give them time to make necessary plans. Be sure to get signed permission from each parent whose child is going on the trip. (See Form 4.5 as an example.)

3. Make arrangements for buses or other transportation at least three months in advance, if possible.

4. Be sure that the appropriate school personnel, especially your principal and the office workers, know in advance about your trip. Put your plans in writing.

5. Give notice to your school dietitian, so the cafeteria can plan for your absence. If asked, the cafeteria might even provide boxed lunches for your students.

6. As soon as you have made arrangements for your field trip, write down all of the specifics and keep the details in a special folder. Be sure to record the trip on your calendar.

7. Use a class checklist to mark off those who have paid or who are not going. You could use several columns to help you make notes regarding individual students.

8. Prepare your students a day or two before your trip. Tell them about some of the things they will see. Introduce any vocabulary words or preliminary knowledge they should know. Some places send information in advance, so teachers can introduce the trip to their students. If attending a play based on a story, read and discuss the story before going. This makes it easier for them to follow along.

9. Be sure that each student has a name tag. It's important that adults in charge can speak to a child using his or her name.

10. If you have parents or volunteers going with you, explain their responsibilities. They like knowing what's expected of them.

11. Sometimes it's a good idea to have your students divided into groups to help adults keep track of them. Divide the students into groups and give the volunteers a list of the students in their group. Their name tag could match the color and shape of the student name tags in their group.

12. If traveling by bus, it is a good idea to have a list of students who are on the trip. Always check the list when boarding the bus. Also, have your students sit in the same seats both

going to and returning from the trip. Have your parents and other volunteers spread throughout the bus to help with any problems that should arise.

13. If you are taking lunches, be sure to have enough boxes or coolers on hand. Parents can bring some from home. Have volunteers arrive in time before the trip to pack the lunches, pass out name tags, and take each group to the restroom. This leaves you time to do other things with your students.

14. Remember to thank your volunteers, bus drivers, and those who directed your field trip. Letters from the children are always more meaningful.

A successful field trip is one where everyone has a good time. Be sure to follow up the next day with a discussion, a game, or a worksheet that reviews what students saw and learned.

Form 4.1

Schedule for 2004–2005 School Year

For Mary Jones, First Grade

8:40–8:50	Homeroom
8:50–9:00	Morning announcements, attendance, lunch count, and calendar
9:00–10:00	Language activity, analogies, and writer's workshop
10:00–11:18	Language arts block—phonics, reading, literature, skills and writing
11:19–11:49	Lunch
11:50–11:55	Bathroom and drinks
11:55–12:25	Small reading group instruction and centers
12:25–1:25	Math
1:25–1:55	Physical education class (teacher's planning period)
1:55–2:15	Small-group instruction and silent reading
2:15–2:40	Science or social studies
2:40	End of the day announcements
2:45	First bell
2:50	Second bell

Course	Day	Time
Art	Thursday	11:55–12:45
Guidance	Thursday*	12:50–1:25
Special Reading Program	Daily	10:45–11:15
Music	Fridays	12:50–1:25
Recess	Daily	12:00–12:15

* Alternating weeks

Form 4.2

Excused Absence Schedule

Special permission to leave class is allowed for these courses for the students listed:

	Monday	Tuesday	Wednesday	Thursday	Friday
Specific learning disability (SLD) students					
Speech and language class					
Gifted class					
ESOL class					
Special reading classes					
Tutoring program					
Chorus/Band					
Clinic visits					

Form 4.3

Substitute Teacher Information

By _____

To My Substitute:

    Thank you so much for agreeing to teach for me today! If possible, please read this booklet, which I prepared for you, before you meet my students. I think that it will help answer many of your questions and provide you with the information necessary for you to enjoy your day.

    A substitute's day begins at _____ and ends at _____.

    Please feel free to leave any comments you might have either in the margin of my lesson plans or in the space provided below. _____ is a colleague of mine who can assist you if you should have any questions.

    Enjoy the students and have a wonderful day!

Sincerely,

_____

Substitute Teacher's Comments / Observations:

_____

_____

_____

_____

_____

_____

_____

_____

_____

_____

_____

_____

_____

Form 4.4

Things a Substitute Needs to Know

1. Please find a map of this school, the daily schedule, a seating chart, and a list of the faculty and staff of this school and their titles in the front pocket of this folder.

2. My lesson plans can be found _____.

3. The teacher manuals are located _____.

4. The class roster for emergencies, such as fire drills, is _____.

5. Here is a list of my most reliable student helpers:

_____   _____

_____   _____

_____   _____

_____   _____

6. The following is a list of students who may require more attention:

_____   _____

_____   _____

_____   _____

_____   _____

7. My discipline plan is:

_____

_____

_____

_____

_____

8. Directions for a fire drill are:

_____

_____

_____

_____

Form 4.4 (continued)

9. Directions for a tornado drill are:

_____

_____

_____

_____

Important: In all emergencies or drills, the teacher in charge is the last one to leave the room. Be sure to take the emergency class roster with you during the drill.

10. Library visitations are as follows:

_____

_____

_____

_____

11. Computers may be used as follows:

_____

_____

_____

_____

12. Centers are used as follows:

_____

_____

_____

_____

13. Lunch begins at _____ and ends at _____. Please be prompt. It normally takes about _____ minutes to quiet down, line up, and walk to the lunchroom.

Form 4.4 (continued)

14. P.E. class is from _____ to _____.

15. Free play or playground time is from _____ to _____.

Comments:

_____

_____

_____

_____

_____

_____

_____

_____

_____

_____

_____

_____

_____

Form 4.5

Field Trip Permission Form

School Name _____

Date _____

Student Name _____

Field Trip Location _____

Date of Trip _____

Method of Transportation

_____ Walking _____ School Bus _____ Rental Vehicle

_____ Private Passenger Car _____ Commercial Carrier _____ Other

Approximate Time and Duration of Field Trip			
Departure		Return	

Parents/Guardians:

To have a safe and successful trip, I ask that you carefully read the following items and mark a checkmark next to each item to show that you understand and agree to each one. *Your child's safety is my main concern on this trip*. It is for this reason that I ask for your understanding and cooperation in returning this permission slip to me as soon as possible.

Thank you.

Sincerely,

_____, *Teacher*

Form 4.5 (continued)

_____ *I authorize school representatives to obtain medical treatment for my child in case of serious illness or injury. I agree to pay for such treatment and/or have my insurance cover it.*

_____ *I understand that the trained school employee who usually dispenses medications may or may not be present during this trip. A responsible staff member will dispense medications.*

_____ *I have written on the lines provided below any instructions/precautions regarding my child's welfare or medications. I have also noted any health-related conditions or allergies that my child has.*

Signature of Parent/Guardian _____

Home Phone _____ *Work Phone* _____ *Other* _____

Alternate Emergency Contact (Name/Relationship) _____

Home Phone _____ *Work Phone* _____ *Other* _____

Lunch Information (to be completed by a parent/guardian):

My child will: _____ bring a bag lunch from home

_____ buy a bag lunch from the school cafeteria

Lunch will be late that day. Please provide your child with a light snack.

5

Discipline and Management of Students

Choosing Your Style of Discipline

Discipline style is a very personal decision; it must correspond with a teacher's personality if it is going to work effectively. The most difficult part of a discipline plan is determining which methods will work for the various types of children that you have.

Children are as varied as the sand in the sea. Some children respond with a simple stern look or stare. Others need a good talking to or a time out. Then, there are those who have to be monitored hour to hour.

Young teachers graduate from colleges and universities filled with exciting new ideas and enthusiasm. They are eager to put all their ideas to work immediately in the classroom. Many are disappointed and shocked when they find that some students will take advantage of them or will be difficult to reach because of their behavior.

Although schools need the refreshing ideas of new teachers, the most important need is to establish the classroom climate in which to introduce these ideas. Classroom rules should be designed to meet the needs of both you and the class. However, make sure they are rules that will work and will be enforced. The worst behavior occurs when good rules are not kept. Rules help teachers earn the respect of the students, which is needed before teaching can begin. Students want an orderly classroom in which everyone has a chance and feels comfortable. If you can establish this comfortable environment for your students, they will feel at ease in learning and in making mistakes. Parents also want to know that their child is in a safe environment with a teacher who will encourage, guide, and protect them.

It is important to remember that you are the teacher, and the students look to you for direction. The students need to know your expectations. If you are ready to start teaching, and two students are not paying attention, then wait. Do not start teaching until you have everyone's attention. Waiting gives all students the message that what you are doing is important. Kindly warn the two students that it is their responsibility to listen, and if they don't, then they will be responsible for the consequences.

Many schools offer various types of discipline programs from which you can study and choose. Pick the one that you feel most comfortable with. Develop it and stick with it. You must believe in that method of discipline if it is going to work. Many new teachers are discouraged and leave teaching after the first year because they started the year with the wrong method of discipline. The biggest mistake new teachers make is wanting to be the students' best friend. Students need to be directed and encouraged to give their best, and the force directing them is the teacher. It is important to have a firm but loving touch. The best rule to remember is to be a teacher first: friendship and respect will follow. If you start off trying to be best friends with your students, you will experience difficulty regaining the authority you need to ensure a successful learning environment.

Some teachers never regain control of their classroom and need to seek outside help. You can request help from the school counselor, principal, or another teacher. Asking for help can be very humiliating, but it is sometimes essential. Loss of classroom control is very real and often happens to new teachers. It is important to be prepared to deal with this problem.

Student-Generated Rules

During the first week of school, you and your students should generate rules. Once you establish a list with your students, it is important that they agree with, vote on, and sign their names at the bottom of the classroom rules. Keep this list posted where it will be seen at all times. When this is done, you will have established the groundwork for your classroom discipline. When students disobey a rule, remind them that this was their rule, not yours, and that it was their decision to disobey it. If the teacher alone made up the rules, students can easily claim the rules are unfair. However, if the students generate the rules, then they have to assume responsibility for them. Students need to know that you expect them to be responsible for their actions.

The hardest part of training students in proper behavior is to teach them to take responsibility for their actions and the skills that enable them to work well with others. If the students can master these skills, then they will be ready to work in teams, which helps promote an exciting classroom atmosphere.

After your class sets the rules needed for a well-run classroom, you can be as creative as you want. It takes time to establish your classroom rules. The first month of school is usually dedicated to implementing structure through rules. It is well worth the time invested because then the rest of the year will run more smoothly.

Table 5.1   Student-Generated Rules

Have respect for other students and their things.	(By Mark)
Walk correctly in line.	(By Madelyn)
Do not talk during class.	(By Brandon)
Always use good manners.	(By Henry)
Do not run in the classroom.	(By Ashley)
Stay in your seat during class.	(By Dante)
Stay on task.	(By Nathan)
Listen carefully.	(By Sheila)

Privileges and Rewards

Students need to realize the importance of rules, but they also like to know they will receive privileges and rewards if they follow the rules. Next to the rules post student-generated ideas for rewards for excellent behavior. Rewards come in all varieties. A reward can be tangible, such as a popcorn or pizza party, pencils, stickers, food, posters, books, and so on. Another fun award is to cook in the classroom. Students love to cook, especially when they know that there might be something to enjoy eating afterward. (You could also teach measurement at the same time and fit it right into your curriculum.) Be careful to check on with school policy before assigning rewards. Some schools have restrictions on tangible rewards. When using food as a reward it is also important to check with parents about allergies.

Many educators prefer activities to reinforce behavior, such as lunch with the teacher, a picnic lunch outside, special no-homework passes, extra computer time, extra recess with another class, extra center time, or designation as the special helper for the day. Some teachers award points toward special privileges or projects. Don't forget that the best awards can be as simple as praise, a wink, or a smile.

Classroom Behavior Code System

One way to objectively grade each student's behavior is to keep track of each individual's behavior throughout the year. Most grade cards, or progress reports, have a space to give a grade for student behavior during the grading period. Some teachers find that using a code helps to keep track of behavior.

The following is an example of a behavior tracking system. Notice the common abbreviations simply denote the area where improvement is needed. You may find different abbreviations work better for you. The key is to find something that you can easily track without becoming distracted.

Table 5.2   Classroom Behavior Tracking

1. Failure to have school supplies each day	**SS** = School Supplies
2. No homework when due	**H** = Homework
3. Not Listening	**L** = Listening
4. Failure to follow directions	**FD** = Following Directions
5. Difficulty staying on task	**T** = Staying on Task
6. Failure to raise hand to speak	**RH** = Raising Hand
7. Not keeping hands, feet, or objects to self	**HFO** = Using Hands, Feet, or Objects
8. Not displaying good manners at all times	**M** = Manners

These codes can be used for grading purposes and to inform parents of their child's behavior. Instead of giving students a checkmark when they misbehave, put the corresponding code letter in your grade book or on a chart along with the date of the infraction. Then, when grading the students' behavior, you will have an objective record to guide you. (*Note:* If you have students who are often or always without school supplies, encourage them to periodically clean out their desks and take inventory of what they have and what they need. See Form 5.1 at the end of this chapter. Keep some of these notes available for the students and encourage them to use them when they are low on supplies.)

Different Types of Children

The Difficult Child

What does a teacher do with a child who does not appear to care about rules or safety? This problem can be a teacher's nightmare and is not uncommon. You may even have more than one difficult child in your classroom. When this happens, it is important to attack the problem immediately. First, try to work with the child by discussing the inappropriate behavior in private. (*Note:* It is important to deal with any behavior issue privately to avoid the child receiving negative attention or being embarrassed.) This tells the student that you mean business.

When a student misbehaves, it is important for the teacher to stay calm and respond immediately. When talking to a student who has misbehaved, stay cool, look the student in the eye, and speak firmly about how disappointed you are that the student is not being responsible for his or her actions. In doing this, you are telling the student you are not angry at the student but at the unacceptable behavior. You are also giving the problem back to the student and asking the student what he or she plans on doing about it. Attending to the misbehavior in this fashion saves time because you are directing your attention at the misbehavior and not allowing for rambling stories to take place.

This type of child at times may need to be isolated from the others in the classroom. When doing so, move the child to a quiet corner or to the side of the room, where the child will not get attention. Encourage the other students not to give any attention to the child when isolated. Instead, praise other students for displaying positive behaviors. This can sometimes be more effective than isolation because the isolated child learns from example. If the behavior is something you feel the class needs to discuss, have the student write his or her name in a notebook for items to be discussed at the next classroom meeting. The secret to disciplining is to do it quickly and effectively and get back to your main task, which is teaching.

It is sometimes difficult to like a child who has behavior problems. However, your job is to find something to like in this type of child. Try all that you can to make the child feel truly appreciated. Showing true friendship is much harder for these children to do, but a teacher can promote this through example.

The Shy Child

Each classroom has a few shy, withdrawn students. They are so quiet that sometimes they are overlooked. It is especially important for a teacher to recognize who these students are and try to make them feel as comfortable as possible. Make sure they get a chance to contribute and share.

Many shy children like to participate in classroom activities; however, they are very insecure and are afraid they will make a mistake and be laughed at by their peers. The teacher must create an atmosphere in the classroom where it is acceptable for someone to make a mistake. The teacher needs to remind the students that we learn and grow with our mistakes, and if a person makes an error, it is fine. This comfort is extremely important if learning is to take place in the classroom.

Another strategy for encouraging shy students is to ask them to be special helpers. Chances are they will be delighted. Assign them to work with sweet, outgoing (not domineering) children, who will help them feel like an important part of the class. You will be amazed how quickly this will work. Some shy students also love to play act. This allows them to show they can be imaginative and creative like the other students.

The Gifted Child

It's always a delight to know that some of your students are gifted. A gifted student in a classroom can be a wonderful role model, especially if they show positive leadership qualities.

However, some gifted students have been told too often how wonderful and smart they are, and they forget there are other students in the classroom. This can pose a problem. Often gifted children feel that they are superior to the other children, and that the rules don't always apply to them. The following behaviors might be expected from gifted students who have a high self-opinion:

- Blurts out answers

- Makes smart-aleck remarks

- Has an overbearing demeanor

- Has to have things their way

- Are not team players

- Do not work well with other students

- Try to correct the teacher

- Feel they are always right, even when they are mistaken

If a gifted student displays any of these behaviors, the teacher can devise a behavior chart to teach the student how to become more cooperative. There may even be times when the teacher has to exclude the gifted student from an activity to make the student understand that the teacher is serious. This can be difficult because you are using behavior modification on students who think they are perfect. Be prepared; this will take patience and time.

The Abused or Neglected Child

Almost always there will be students in your classroom who come to school with an unkempt appearance. Their hair is shaggy, and their clothes are often wrinkled or dirty. You will be able to tell the difference between the poorer child, who comes in clean, from the unkempt child, who is not properly cared for. It is important to keep a close eye on these children. It is possible they come from abusive home situations.

Some teachers plan a special hygiene unit in health to teach the importance of cleanliness. If your school is fortunate enough to have a school nurse, perhaps he or she could arrange a health lesson for your class. Sometimes local public health agencies provide speakers for classrooms on this subject.

It's always important to gather background information on these students. Ask the counselor or principal for any information about the family. Perhaps the school's social worker could help you, also. It is also important that you document anything unusual that you notice or any concerns you might have and follow up on these incidents.

Many times it is the unkempt child that has the problem with lice, sores, bites, and other health issues. Students cannot learn if they are hungry, uncomfortable, or not well. It is up to the teacher to help these children in any way possible.

The Bully

Even if you escape having a bully in your classroom, chances are you will have to deal with one in the future. A bully comes in many guises: boy or girl of any color, tall or short, heavy or slight, low intelligence to gifted, wealthy or poor. How do you recognize a bully? Watch for the child who has to be first and does so by elbowing his or her way to the front of the line. Bullies want to be in control. They usually try to dominate every situation, even if they do not know what they are doing. They love being in power and don't care who they step on to get where they are going. Most of us have known bullies and can recognize them immediately.

How do you handle a bully? First, make sure the student understands that the classroom rules are for everyone. Next, explain to the bully that blaming others for his or her behavior will not be allowed. Be firm and fair and make sure this child understands why he or she is being reprimanded. Bullies like to test teachers, so it is important to be firm and follow through with any consequences. Many times a bully is insecure and uses power to hide insecurities. It is important to recognize bullies and help them become team players. Many times you will have to isolate these students or take away privileges, such as recess.

Bullies are usually resistant, so do not expect the problem to be solved after a few reprimands. Sometimes it takes most of the school year to overcome bullying behavior. A teacher has to be patient and understanding, even when it would be much easier to send the child to the principal or to isolation in another classroom. Remember, the student will have to come back to your classroom, so you still need to deal with the problem. It is best to attempt to handle issues yourself and use outside action as the last resort.

The Child Who Lies

It is difficult when a teacher has to confront a student who lies. Students lie for many different reasons. Some like to enhance their stories to give them a feeling of importance. Others do it because they are afraid of getting into trouble if they tell the truth. Some students lie to protect peers. Others are angry or jealous and are trying to be accepted by their peers at any cost. Then there are those who do it so they can get what they want and do not care who they injure along the way.

The saddest consequence of students lying is loss of trust. If a student lies, consult outside help. First, call the parents for a conference. If the conference doesn't work, ask your guidance counselor to work with the student. The problem may be more serious than you realize; for example, the student may require psychological help. When working with a student who has a major problem, make sure you keep your principal alerted as to what is happening. You will need the principal's support if a problem arises.

The Shunned or Antisocial Child

A teacher works with many challenging personalities; however, the shunned or antisocial child is one of the most difficult. These students are suffering inside and do not know how to cope. The shunned student often becomes more antisocial, and this behavior leads to anger and the desire to lash out and blame others. You need to be aware of these students and try to find ways of helping them.

These students are very recognizable. They are the last to be chosen to join a team. They are usually the ones the other students do not want to work with on a project. No one wants to sit with or near them. Although society has chosen to ignore these students, it is necessary to try to help them learn to interact successfully with their peers. First, be kind to these children and make sure that your students know that they have special problems. Let the other students know they must work together with the shunned child. Be firm about this. Usually there are students who are dependable. Ask those students if they would be your helpers and work with the problem students. Be sure to provide the helpers and the shunned children a lot of understanding, and watch the groups closely.

Antisocial students are often their own worst enemy. They do not feel capable of doing anything right and lash out at others when frustrated. Their self-esteem is low. It is difficult for them to make friends. Many times when they do befriend another student, it is with someone who is inclined to get into trouble. Be watchful and aware because this student might need professional help. Again, involve the parents, the counselor and nurse, and, your principal.

Classroom Meetings

Sometimes classroom meetings or discussions can be beneficial. It is important for the teacher to be a guiding force at these class meetings while allowing the students to voice their opinions. The teacher needs to make sure the students understand that no cruel or unsafe actions will be allowed in the classroom.

Many classrooms have a short student-run meeting at some point during the day. Some teachers start the day with a 10–15-minute meeting to set the tone for the day and to remind the students of their goals. If a student is constantly taking away from class time because of a behavior problem, have the other students discuss in an orderly fashion how they can help the student in a positive way. When the student who is misbehaving realizes the rest of the class is not going to put up with the misbehavior, most of the time the reaction will be to try harder to behave appropriately.

However, if the misbehavior continues, it is possible that the students might suggest a punishment that fits the misbehavior. This is when it is especially important that the teacher be the guiding force. It is your duty to make sure all decision-making stays fair and balanced.

Before the meeting is over, it is important to take a minute to recognize good behavior in the classroom. If students realize that good behavior and kind deeds are recognized each day, then they will try harder to do their best. Recognition can be given to individuals or to the whole class. Students love to be recognized and will respond to positive comments.

The classroom meetings show the importance of working together. The message is made clear to the students that cooperative actions make learning happen in the classroom. The following examples illustrate when to send a student out of the classroom during a class meeting.

Example

Once, after a rather lengthy winter break, a fourth grade student named Sandy came into class looking quite pale. She was wearing a colorful bandana on her head. The teacher could see that some of the other students were laughing among themselves at the strange hat that their classmate was wearing. Her mother, who informed the teacher that Sandy was recuperating from surgery, accompanied her. Her hair had to be shaved off before surgery; thus, she was wearing the strange-looking bandana. The teacher knew that this could present a problem for Sandy, so she decided to take action before any emotional damage could occur.

The teacher arranged to have Sandy go to the school nurse for a predetermined amount of time. She then called a class meeting with the rest of the students. She told them exactly what had happened to Sandy. A discussion was started on how the students thought she might feel with the strange-looking bandana on her head. She let each student share his or her thoughts and feelings. Then they discussed how they could make Sandy feel better. Ideas were shared and written on the board.

Before it was time for Sandy to return to class, they had come up with a plan to help her feel better while recuperating. Each day someone would be in charge of being her special friend and helper. They would sit with her in class, during lunch, or any other special activity outside the classroom. They would think of kind ways to make her feel better and assure her that she was a valued member of the class. Sandy did not know what went on during her absence from the classroom, but from that moment she felt comfortable with her situation.

Many years later, Sandy was working as a cashier at a local grocery store. One day her fourth grade teacher happened to go through her cashier's line. Sandy remembered her teacher after so many years and recalled the kindness that she had received that year.

Example

One morning, as Billy came into the classroom, the teacher could tell he was upset by the expression on his face and by the way he was walking.

Billy hung up his jacket and backpack after taking out some supplies, but he did not remove his cap. He then went to his desk.

Since there was still time before opening activities, the teacher called Billy up to her desk. She reminded him that he would need to remove his cap before the pledge of allegiance and the national anthem. She was about to ask him if he wanted to talk about what was upsetting him when he said, "Please, don't make me take it off!"

Billy explained to the teacher that his parents had discovered lice nits in his hair. To take care of the problem, they shaved his head. He told his teacher that he was embarrassed and felt like he looked awful. He was afraid that the class would laugh at him if he took his cap off.

The teacher told Billy that she understood and that he could keep his hat on. Billy was very relieved but worried that someone would ask why he was the only one allowed to keep his cap on.

The teacher replied that she would explain that Billy had special permission to keep his cap on. She then told him that, if he felt comfortable enough later on that day, he could try removing his cap. She promised she would make sure that no one laughed.

The morning proceeded in a normal way until the time when Billy left the class for an hour to attend a learning disabilities class.

The teacher thought this would be the perfect time to discuss Billy's problem in a class meeting. She asked everyone to stop working and to go back to their desks and give her their undivided attention.

When she had everyone's attention, the teacher explained that she would need their help in solving a special problem, and she wanted them to listen and think very carefully.

She then explained Billy's dilemma to them and asked everyone to try to put themselves into Billy's place. She told them to close their eyes and think of how they might feel if they were in Billy's place. After a couple of minutes of silence, the teacher asked them to share their feelings. Several children explained that they would feel different, lonely, sad, mad, upset, stupid, and embarrassed. The teacher replied that Billy felt all these things, too.

She explained that Billy might want to remove his cap later. They all agreed to be respectful of his feelings and promised not to laugh. She had them raise their hands and promise her that they would go on working normally if Billy decided to remove his hat. She had them say aloud that they promised not to laugh.

That afternoon Billy felt hot and asked the teacher if he could remove his cap. He slowly did so, while looking around at his classmates. All the children went on normally with their activities, and no one laughed. So Billy kept his cap off until dismissal time. The teacher sent everyone home with a special sticker for working hard and treating each other with kindness.

The next day, when Billy came into the classroom, he got out some supplies and his homework and hung up his jacket . . . and his cap.

The following example illustrates when a student should be present during a class meeting.

Example

Charles was well liked by most of the students in his class. However, he thought he could use this to his advantage and continuously misbehave. Because the students liked him, they were uncertain about how to address his misbehavior. They would either ignore it or nervously giggle at it. The teacher saw what was happening and tried to deal with it on a one-to-one basis, so she didn't embarrass Charles. When it became apparent that this was not going to work, she called in his parents. It wasn't long before they realized he was going to need a behavior chart to monitor his actions in the classroom. Each day, before going home, the teacher would fill out the chart with Charles, so he would know why it was marked accordingly. Then the chart would go home to be reviewed and signed by the parents. The next day it was returned to the teacher. (See forms at the end of this chapter.) Even though his behavior in the classroom improved, the students in the class were becoming upset because Charles's behavior was affecting their privileges in other areas of the school, such as P.E. and art class and the lunchroom.

Finally, the teacher decided to have a class meeting, with Charles present, to discuss his behavior. The meeting was carefully run to be *constructive* rather than *destructive*. The teacher emphasized that the discussion should be about Charles's actions rather than about him personally. She modeled her expectations by giving examples of appropriate phrases, such as "When you _____, it makes me feel _____"; "I feel angry when you _____"; and "I feel cheated when the whole class misses _____ because of your actions." (This could also be effective as a role-play situation.)

When it became apparent how the students really felt, Charles was shocked. He was surprised to hear his friends telling how disappointed they were in his behavior and that they wished he would care enough to think of them once in awhile.

When the meeting was over, Charles knew that his peers were not going to put up with his behavior, but he felt they still liked him and were willing to help him in any way they could. This was what Charles really needed to hear. He refused to listen to adults, but he did react to his peers. Having Charles's actions discussed at a class meeting with him present turned out to be a positive and ideal situation. Although Charles continued to work on his problems, he did have some lapses. But he did not give up because he realized his peers were still watching.

Isolation

If you find that a problem student is not responding, and learning is being compromised, then you might want to ask an experienced teacher to help you. Sometimes children need to know that you mean business by isolating them in another teacher's classroom corner. The isolation can be prearranged, and the child should always be monitored. It is interesting, however, that children who misbehave do not like being isolated from their classroom.

What happens when isolation does not appear to be working? This is not an uncommon problem. At this point, it is time to call the parents and have a meeting. Many times parents see the same problems at home and are frustrated also. Working together, you might suggest a Weekly Behavior/Work Calendar (see Form 5.2), which is a way for the teacher and parents to track the child's behavior. If the student has a successful week, the parents could have a reward system at home, something simple like extra time on the computer or having a friend over after school. If the student lapses, some privilege would then be revoked. A behavior chart can be useful if both the parents and the teacher implement it. The key is consistency—following up and staying on top of the problem. If either the teacher or the parents neglect their part in following up, it will not work.

If you feel a student will not reap the benefits of a behavior chart, you might consider having another staff member, such as a school nurse, guidance counselor, principal, or teacher observe the child in the classroom. You might also want to suggest to the parents that they consult with their child's doctor for a physical. It is not unusual for a behavioral problem to stem from a health-related cause.

Another route to take are the use of forms, which can be found at the end of this chapter. For example, if you have removed a student to a quiet area, you could have him or her reflect on the inappropriate behavior by writing an action plan for you (Form 5.3). This plan can be between you and the student or you can send it home to be signed by the parent. If the behavior persists or worsens, you could send a discipline notice (Form 5.4) home to involve the parents. Finally, if all else fails, a referral to the principal (Form 5.5) might be in order, depending on the severity of the problem. It is imperative that the students know you expect their best behavior so that learning will take place for all children in the classroom.

On a more positive note, students need feedback each day to teach them the importance of good behavior. One way a teacher can do this is by stapling a monthly calendar in a pocket folder for each child and using it as a communication source between the parents and the teacher (see Form 5.6). The pockets of the folder can hold memos or letters going back and forth between parents and teacher. If the student has a good day at school, put a checkmark or stamp in that day's box. If the student has a problem at school, write a quick note in the box letting the parent know the nature of the problem. Should the problem become severe, write a quick note to let the parent know that you will be calling tonight (or "Please contact me at school," or "A conference is needed"). Students need to be aware that you are the guiding force and that you expect them to be responsible for their actions. Knowing their folders will be looked at each day by their parents will help them to realize the importance of good behavior.

Using Humor in the Classroom

Humor in the classroom can work to your advantage to help diffuse sticky situations. It is important to show children that it is acceptable to make mistakes and even more important to be able to laugh at them. Many times difficult children have a problem with this. They become irritated because they feel their peers are laughing at them. If this is the case, the teacher can present a lesson about the appropriate use of humor. It is necessary for children with problems to realize that their peers are not laughing at them but with them; there is a big difference between the two. To avoid hurting other students' feelings, a teacher must insist that the class not laugh at each other's mistakes.

Students learn from their teachers. If teachers create humorous situations from their mistakes, then most of the time students will follow these actions. For example, if the teacher misspells a word in front of the class and a student catches it, the teacher could respond by saying, "Oh, no! Besides bad hair, the weather has affected my spelling!"

Humor handled correctly can help lighten the pressure in delicate situations. Consider the following example where humor was used:

> At recess one day, Jane fell into a puddle. One of the children said it looked like she wet her pants. Poor Jane was horrified! She cried and cried. The teacher asked a dependable child to take Jane to the nurse's office to get a change of clothes. Quietly, she removed the rude child and talked to him about being more considerate with words that would not embarrass others.
>
> After recess, the teacher had the children sit in a circle for story time. Before she started to read the story, she told the children about a time she was riding her horse in a big city July Fourth parade, and her pants ripped in the back. She told them how upset she felt and how embarrassed she was and that it ruined her whole day. Her brother made fun of her and told all of his friends. Luckily, her sister let her borrow a sweater to tie around her waist and cover her backside. It was interesting to see that most of her students listened with sincerity, while a handful started to laugh at the situation. She reiterated that even now, many years later, when she thought back on it, it brought back a sad memory. She pointed out that one rude comment made in haste can stay with you the rest of your life, and that is why it is so important to say only kind things to others. She finished telling the students that no one in this world has the right to make another person miserable by saying unkind remarks. She told them if her brother had not made fun of her and had helped her instead, she probably would have laughed about it later and it wouldn't have ruined her day.

Another situation in which humor was used concerns a teacher who backed up to the chalkboard and mistakenly rubbed against it. She didn't realize that part of a sentence had been transferred to the seat of her pants. A very kind student came forward and whispered in the teacher's ear, "Mrs. Smith, you have a sentence on your rear." The teacher turned around and responded, "Oh, no! It's a good thing you told me, or I would have walked around all day with people trying to read my rear." The teacher brushed the sentence off her backside and together she and the student laughed with the rest of the class. The incident turned into a positive, humorous moment shared by everyone.

It's important to teach children that many times you know instinctively when to laugh or not to laugh. If you are in doubt, don't laugh. It is the safer choice. Humor, when used correctly, can make a classroom fun and cushion a lot of uncomfortable situations. Try implementing it in your discipline plan whenever you can.

After your first year, you may find it necessary to reevaluate your ideas to fit each new class. New personalities might require changes in your plan. Remember, you are the guiding force and ultimately responsible for the learning environment in your classroom. At the same time, keep a positive attitude, stay calm, develop a sense of humor, and promote feelings of self-worth and success.

Form 5.1

Request for Supplies

Dear _____ :

My school supplies are running low. Please help me remember to get these supplies. I need the following:

_____ Pencils
_____ Crayons
_____ Eraser
_____ Glue sticks
_____ Spiral notebook
_____ Scissors
_____ Washable markers
_____ Other: _____

Thank you!
Love,

_____

Dear _____ :

My school supplies are running low. Please help me remember to get these supplies. I need the following:

_____ Pencils
_____ Crayons
_____ Eraser
_____ Glue sticks
_____ Spiral notebook
_____ Scissors
_____ Washable markers
_____ Other: _____

Thank you!
Love,

_____

Dear _____ :

My school supplies are running low. Please help me remember to get these supplies. I need the following:

_____ Pencils
_____ Crayons
_____ Eraser
_____ Glue sticks
_____ Spiral notebook
_____ Scissors
_____ Washable markers
_____ Other: _____

Thank you!
Love,

_____

Dear _____ :

My school supplies are running low. Please help me remember to get these supplies. I need the following:

_____ Pencils
_____ Crayons
_____ Eraser
_____ Glue sticks
_____ Spiral notebook
_____ Scissors
_____ Washable markers
_____ Other: _____

Thank you!
Love,

_____

Weekly Behavior/Work Calendar

Name: _____

Week of: _____

Monday	Classwork Completed? _____	On Task? _____	Behavior _____	Homework Completed? _____	Homework Assigned: _____	Parent's Initials _____
Tuesday	Classwork Completed? _____	On Task? _____	Behavior _____	Homework Completed? _____	Homework Assigned: _____	Parent's Initials _____
Wednesday	Classwork Completed? _____	On Task? _____	Behavior _____	Homework Completed? _____	Homework Assigned: _____	Parent's Initials _____
Thursday	Classwork Completed? _____	On Task? _____	Behavior _____	Homework Completed? _____	Homework Assigned: _____	Parent's Initials _____
Friday	Classwork Completed? _____	On Task? _____	Behavior _____	Homework Completed? _____	Homework Assigned: _____	Parent's Initials _____

Teacher / Parent Comments:

_____

_____

Key: V = Very Good S = Satisfactory N = Needs Improvement U = Unsatisfactory N/A = Not Applicable

Form 5.3

Student–Teacher Contract

Name: _____   Date: _____

ACTION PLAN

I will stop:

_____
_____
_____

Because:

_____
_____
_____

I will begin:

_____
_____
_____

To change my behavior, I will try:

_____
_____

Signed by:

Student   **Teacher**

_____   _____

Form 5.4

Discipline Notice to Parents

Dear Parents,

This note is to inform you that your child, _____, is experiencing difficulty in one or more of the areas listed below. To have a quality education, it is important that every child conform to the rules and regulations that have been set up in our classroom and school. Please have a talk with your child so he or she can develop better self-discipline in the indicated areas.

Thank you for taking the time to do this. Together, we are partners in your child's education.

Sincerely,

_____

Teacher

- -

Your child needs to <u>improve</u> in the following areas:

_____ *Listening and/or following directions*
_____ *Having necessary supplies (paper, textbooks, pencils, etc.)*
_____ *Using time wisely*
_____ *Using manners/socializing with others*
_____ *Completing assignments*
_____ *Completing/turning in homework*
_____ *Bringing unacceptable items*
_____ *Disturbing/interrupting others*
_____ *Being absent/tardy too frequently*
_____ *Getting up and out of desk too often*
_____ *Being aggressive on school grounds (pushing, hitting, talking back)*
_____ *Other:* _____

_____

<u>Please sign and return this sheet.</u>

Parent Signature: _____
Date Signed: _____
Daytime Phone: _____

Thank you for your concern and cooperation!

Form 5.5

Referral Note to Principal

Student: _____

Date: _____

    The student named above has been disrupting our class by the following actions checked below. I have tried at least three alternative measures of discipline to change this child's actions to be more conducive to a successful learning environment. Please speak to the child concerning this matter.

    Thank you,

_____ ,

____ Classroom Teacher   ____ Specialist

Behaviors:

____ Disruptive in class   ____ Using improper language

____ Verbally abusing others   ____ Physically abusing others

____ Disrespecting classmate   ____ Failing to follow directions

____ Disrespecting teacher   ____ Failing to complete assignment

____ Defacing school property   ____ Other

Course(s):

____ Physical Education   ____ Music

____ Art   ____ Guidance

____ Homeroom   ____ Other

Explanation (to be completed by teacher):

_____

_____

_____

_____

Action taken (to be filled out by principal or acting administrator):

_____

_____

_____

_____

_____

_____

_____

Form 5.6

Monthly Calendar

Monday	Tuesday	Wednesday	Thursday	Friday	Notes

6

Conferencing and Working with Parents

Keeping Parents Informed

Parents can be great assets to a teacher, or they can cause major problems. When parents and teachers work together for the good of a child, the child is doubly enriched. When you allow parents to be involved and informed, you are making them feel needed and welcomed. They become a part of the child's educational team.

It is important to connect with your students' parents soon after school begins. Most parents want to be involved in their child's school life: they want to know how their child is doing in school and welcome any constructive suggestions that you might have. You may make your first contact with parents by writing an introductory letter either before the school year begins or soon after the students arrive. Another way to help make parents feel connected is to call them to introduce yourself. If you make contact early in the school year, you can usually say something positive about each child.

Classroom Newsletters

Classroom newsletters should be sent home periodically throughout the year, with a minimum of three or four per year. It's nice to send one at each grading period, so you can discuss the subject matter that class learned that particular period. Parents need to know what is being taught in school, so they can provide more support at home. Include some ways in which your parents can help at home. Also include information about any field trips you have planned. If you are thorough in your newsletters, you will be spared from later having to send home notes or answer parents' questions about a certain activity. You might also include a calendar for any upcoming events that might be of interest to parents.

Your classroom newsletter is also a great place to thank parents for their help. They will feel appreciated when they see their names mentioned in the classroom news. This promotes good feelings and encourages them to be involved in their child's education.

Your message should express a positive attitude. If you want to talk about a problem, be sure that it is common to most of the students. Then, mention it only after you have mentioned positive things. In other words, work into it gradually. Before you send a newsletter home, be sure to have it proofed and edited by someone who will catch any errors that you might have made. Your newsletters are a reflection of you, so they should be professional and error-free.

Choosing a name or logo for your newsletter allows you to use the same heading throughout the year. Save a copy of the heading, so you can access it quickly and begin writing your next letter home without having to retype the heading. Some computers even have suggested headings for educational newsletters. Keep a copy of each newsletter on your computer, so the next year you can use the newsletter again, with a few changes.

Make your first newsletter simple by introducing yourself and giving useful information parents might need. Be sure to portray yourself in a positive way, so parents feel comfortable having their child in your classroom. Give parents practical suggestions and information, such as the spelling test schedule, the classroom rules, the time lunch is scheduled, the homework policy, a list of school supplies, and the date of Open House. You might have a section at the end of your newsletter where parents sign up to volunteer. Don't make that first letter too long, though. There are many other papers that go home at the beginning of the year, and parents can become overwhelmed, just like your students. Once the first classroom newsletter has gone home, it is a good idea to call some parents to find out if it was received.

Telephoning Parents

The telephone is a wonderful way to communicate with parents. It is quick and personal and doesn't depend on a child to get a note home. Some fortunate teachers have a telephone in their classroom; if you do not, you'll need to use a school phone or your home phone. To save time, you should have each of your students' home and their parents' work phone numbers in your grade book or another handy place. If a student is experiencing extreme problems, you might give your home telephone  number to the child's parent, to help maintain two-way communication. Consider carefully whether you want parents to have your personal telephone number before you give it out.

If you see a problem developing with a student and you contact the child's parents, be sure to start the conversation with something positive about the child. Parents will be impressed with a teacher who notices the positive aspects of their child and will be more understanding about your concerns. This will help you later if you need their cooperation.

E-mail Updates

Another way of keeping in touch that does not require as much of your personal time is to use e-mail. You can use school or your home e-mail. Many teachers feel that their life outside of the classroom should not be invaded with school-related issues, so they do not give out their home e-mail. Indeed, they have this right to privacy during their time away from school. Again, this is a personal decision you will need to make.

Classroom/School Web Sites

Some teachers have their own classroom Web site. These teachers post the day's homework assignment or information about upcoming events so that parents or students can check the information without having to call them. If you choose this way of communicating with parents, then you must keep the site up-to-date. Only general class information should be shared on the Web site. To discuss individual students, send a private e-mail, make a telephone call, or arrange for a conference. A Web site should not be your only form of communication, however, because some parents may not have access to a computer at home.

Parent Conferences

Each year you will be expected to have conferences with your students' parents concerning the academic, social, and emotional progress of their children. Learning how to hold a good conference is one of the most important and necessary skills a teacher possesses.

It is important that the teacher be available for parent-requested conferences and also be able to request conferences in a warm, friendly way. A Conference Request Form (Form 6.1) as well as a Conference Reminder Form (Form 6.2) can be prepared in advance to ask for and to remind parents of an upcoming conference (see forms at the end of this chapter). It's a good idea to place the school's phone number on the request and reminder forms, so parents can call if they need to change the date or time of the conference.

If you have a parent who is particularly reluctant to have a conference and does not respond to your note, a direct phone call with a choice of several conference times and dates may be the best alternative.

If a parent agrees to attend the conference, then prior to the conference date, send home the Conference Reminder Form. Many parents work outside the home and have busy schedules. It's easy to forget a conference in the hubbub of their daily activities. The Conference Reminder Form helps keep parents from forgetting conferences and having to reschedule.

Be prepared for the conference. Have samples of the child's work, scores, tests, and anything else pertinent on the table and ready to show the parents. Doing so lets the parents know that you are well prepared and that this conference was organized to meet its purpose. Many schools provide a student information form, which teachers prepare before the conference (you may want to use one of the forms [6.3 or 6.4] provided at the end of this chapter). This form helps you organize your thoughts ahead of time and also provides written documentation of the conference.

When the parents come into the classroom, take time to shake their hands, make eye contact, and tell them how glad you are that they came. Many teachers assume that parents enjoy coming to conferences. It would be wonderful if every parent felt this way, but, unfortunately, many feel something is wrong and that they are going to hear bad news. Because of this, they may enter the room with their defenses up, ready to take action. Greeting parents in a friendly and sincere way helps them to relax.

Invite the parents to sit at a table. Many teachers have parents sit in front of their desk. Without meaning to, the parents are immediately put into a subordinate position, which is a putdown. Sitting at a table where it is comfortable to show the child's work and talk makes the parents feel they are at the same level as the teacher. This helps them to speak more freely about their child.

Behavior Concerns

Always start a conference by telling the parents about their child's strengths, which parents feel are a reflection of their efforts. Then, if you have some disturbing news about their child, it can be presented by starting with a phrase such as, "Now let's talk about how we can make your child's year successful."

Some of the following phrases might help you get started:

• "An area I would like to see strengthened is . . ."

• "What I have noticed about his relationship to his classmates is . . ."

- "Something I noticed is . . ."

- "One area that concerns me is . . ."

- "I would like to see her do more in the area of . . ."

- "I am encouraged about . . ."

Remember to keep your emotions in check. If you act angry, the parents will become defensive, and the intended benefit of the conference will be lost. (*Note:* If you have reason to believe that the conference might be hostile, be prepared. Ask your principal, guidance counselor, school nurse, or even another teacher to sit in on the conference with you. It is unfortunate to anticipate a negative situation, but sometimes it happens. Having an extra person there helps to diffuse an explosive situation.)

Sometimes it is necessary for the child to attend the conference. This is especially true if there are concerns about the child's behavior. This arrangement allows parents to hear about the child's behavior from the child, as well as the teacher. It also lets the child know that there will be cooperation between the home and school.

Keep the conference open and friendly. In doing so, parents might confide that they see the same behavior or insecurity at home and will ask for or offer to help. You can then brainstorm how you will work together to fix the problem. Many teachers use a simple behavior plan for monitoring a child's behavior. (See form 5.2.) If you and the parents decide to use a behavior plan, it should be simple and involve the child. Check either *N* for "needs improvement," *S* for "satisfactory," or *V* for "very good." Always leave a place for the parents to initial daily, so you know they are monitoring the behavior.

The parent should sign and retain a copy of the conference form. Always ask parents if they have any further questions, or if they would like to add any comments to the form.

Academic Concerns

If the student's problem is academic, brainstorm ways to get extra help. The following are some suggestions to address academic problems:

- *Math*—Fill baggies with flash cards and have them ready to send home.

- *Reading*—Fill baggies with selections of out-of-adoption books from an older series, which is not being used. Show parents how to ask comprehension questions and help their child sound out words.

- *Extra Help*—Have a list of tutors available if the parents ask for and are willing to pay for one.

Telephone Conferences

It is not uncommon to have parents who work two jobs, or whose work hours do not allow time for on-site school conferences. When this happens, try to accommodate them by finding a time to confer on the phone. Gather copies of their child's work, test scores, and behavior information and write up a conference form to send home with the child before the phone conference. As you talk, the parent can follow along. Be sure to ask the parent if he or she has any questions or information to add. If everything is agreeable, ask the parent to sign the conference sheet, keep one copy, and return the original the next day. (*Note:* The envelope containing the conference papers for the phone conference is very important. Always let the student know how important it is that his or her parents get the package. Keep special rewards, such as stickers and pencils, in your desk drawer to give to the student when the envelope is returned.)

It is also necessary to hold frequent conferences with parents whose children are having difficulties. Staying on top of problems is essential. Don't forget to confer with parents of children who are doing well. You may want to suggest testing for gifted programs.

Problem Parents

Many times new teachers are disillusioned when they realize that some parents do not agree with their advice. This makes it difficult for communication between the parents and the teacher. Instead of being upset, be prepared for such an event.

If you are having a problem with a student and finding it difficult to convince the parent to help you, start keeping a folder on this child and document everything: keep track of every time a note is sent home (be sure each note is dated), any response from the parent, notes about telephone calls and conferences, and anything else pertaining to this child.

When documenting events, it is important to jot down objective notes about the child in class, at recess, in the lunchroom, or in the bathrooms. Many times children go home with stories that are misunderstood by the parents. The parent may not confront you until weeks later. By then, when confronted by the parent, you may not recall the situation. Having it written down helps jog your memory and serves to inform the parent.

If an accident occurs, fill out an accident report. You will need to know what caused the incident and who will be responsible for signing the report, if another teacher was present at the time of the accident. Always document your communications with the parents. Even if you have a short chat before, during, or after school, write a quick note about it. These notes are valuable in situations where your actions are questioned by a parent.

Consider the following example concerning a teacher who had a child in her classroom who screamed if things did not go her way. If anyone even touched the child, she would scream. Her teacher worked with the child on this problem and was starting to make progress.

Unfortunately, the home situation was not conducive to firm and loving discipline. The child came from a broken home. Her father was raising her with the help of his sister. His sister had a son who was always in trouble at school and had problems respecting his peers and figures of authority.

About midway through the school year, the little girl's aunt insisted on driving for one of the school field trips. The teacher was surprised but happy that the aunt took an interest in her niece's school events. However, since this was unusual, she wrote a note to herself about it in the margin of her lesson plan book next to that day's date.

The next day, the aunt brought in banana bread that she had baked especially for the teacher. Although delighted, the teacher was somewhat puzzled and suspicious by this sudden act of kindness. Her instincts felt something was amiss and wrote a quick note again in her lesson plan book.

About two weeks later, her principal came to the teacher's classroom with an accident report he wanted her to fill out. He informed her that the little girl's aunt had called the school and claimed her niece was injured in this teacher's class. She stated that one of the other students had thrown a pencil, which landed on her niece's arm. She indicated that the lead had broken off in the child's arm and that surgery would be necessary to have it removed.

The teacher immediately was aware that something was very wrong. With her documentation, she was able to shed light on the unusual attention this aunt had given her. The unusual attention, along with the child's screaming behavior, made the injury report even more questionable. The teacher asked the principal to return later for a walk through her classroom, so he could see where the children were sitting. He did so and instantly agreed with the teacher that the story was fabricated. The niece sat in the back of the room, and the child who was being accused was seated in the front. It was highly unlikely that a pencil could have been thrown with enough force to embed lead into the child's arm.

The truth eventually became clear: the niece's cousin had stabbed her with a pencil at home, and the aunt thought they could sue or make the school responsible for medical damages.

The principal informed the student's family of the teacher's documentation. He also stated that he believed the pencil-throwing incident did not occur in the teacher's classroom. The family backed down from their accusation, thanks to the documentation and questioning attitude of the teacher and a very supportive principal.

If you feel you need assistance in dealing with a difficult parent, take the student documentation folder and share it with your principal. Remember that you are not alone in handling problem parents. Usually, when parents realize that the teacher has documentation, they proceed cautiously or stop bothering the teacher. Many times it's just a communication problem, and once it is addressed, the problem is solved.

Record keeping is not only valuable in situations with difficult parents but will also be part of your evaluation by your principal. The principal will appreciate your efforts, and it will be noted. Principals like knowing that their teachers are efficient. This makes their job easier when working with difficult parents.

Using Parents and Volunteers Wisely

A teacher's job can be overwhelming at times. There is always the worry of how to meet the needs of students who require individual help. One way to help yourself and your students and to involve parents and senior citizens is to create a volunteer program. At the beginning of the year, you might be asked if you would like volunteers in your classroom. With all you have to do at that time, it is easy to say, "Let me think about it." Instead, think about it ahead of time and be ready to accept the offer. Decide which organization you want your classroom to have. Also determine which volunteer jobs parents and organization members can do.

Think of ways that volunteers can best help you. Teachers often feel they can't address all the needs of all of their students. Turn this frustration into a positive by asking for volunteers. If you fall behind in the grading of homework, see if there is a stay-at-home mom who can help you. If it is small group instruction that seems impossible to achieve, train some volunteers by having them observe you. You will be amazed how well such volunteers can help. What is important is to periodically take some time and reflect on how your classroom could be better if you included parents and volunteers. You will feel better knowing that more of your students' needs are being met. It takes some time to set things up and teach volunteers and parents what needs to be done, but once it is done, you will reap the benefits. The following is a list of ideas that can help you decide where you can use a parent or volunteer.

1. Tutoring (reading, writing, and math)

   • Read individually with students

   • Read with small groups

   • Check vocabulary

   • Review math facts

   • Work on math skills

   • Practice handwriting

   • Encourage struggling students to write

   • Help edit individual stories

   • Work with students who have been absent frequently

2. Grading papers (at home or at school)

3. Driving for field trips

4. Chaperoning for field trips

5. Mentoring

6. Organizing and maintaining classroom centers

7. Organizing and setting up class parties

8. Organizing materials for class projects

9. Working with small groups on class projects

10. Wrapping presents for the students

11. Creating displays of students' work

12. Organizing closet space and bookcases

13. Helping with inventory

14. Doing clerical work

15. Changing bulletin boards

16. Typing students' stories on the computer

17. Helping students on the computer

18. Helping students create parent gifts

19. Helping with end-of-the-year packing up

20. Making copies

21. Monitoring student test taking, if allowed

22. Encouraging students to complete work

23. Reading stories to the class or to small groups

Classroom Parties

After scanning your Open House signup sheets, you will have a good idea of which parents would like to help with classroom parties. The times for these parties are generally designated by your school district: before the winter holidays, on Valentine's Day, or at the end of the year.

It's a good idea to meet with interested parents early in the first semester, so you can communicate your ideas and suggestions to the group. They, in turn, will have plenty of time to get organized. Ask the parents to attend an informal meeting in your classroom. Have everyone sit at a table where the group can easily talk. If the parents want to take notes, be sure to have paper and pencils available. Start by telling the parents why you have invited them to your classroom and thank them for volunteering to help. Let them know that you consider their help invaluable.

If a parent would like to serve as room parent, that would be very helpful to you, also. A room parent can save you a great deal of time by phoning other interested parents before each party and letting them know about their party responsibilities.

You might want to tell the parents that you would like to leave the specifics of organization up to them. You should have a handout indicating each party date, along with general party suggestions (plates, cups, napkins, and utensils; refreshments, such as drinks and food items; favors (optional) for each student). If the suggestions are general, the parents can come up with more specific ideas. It's also a good idea to communicate some of the ideas and preparations that were made in the past.

Here are some suggestions for a classroom party:

• It's usually a good idea to have only one or two choices of drinks available.

• If cookies, cupcakes, or small cakes are sent in, they must be store bought (not made at home) to satisfy health requirements. Again, one or two choices are enough. (*Note:* Be sure that your parents understand that no religious emphasis is allowed on cakes or other party items in most public schools.)

• Favors are optional, but many parents like to send goody bags for each child.

• If a large cake or cookie is provided, have a parent precut it for you.

• Enlist one or two parents to help at each party. The parents can take turns attending parties, if necessary. If parents are not available, the children can help you.

• It is wonderful if parents agree to help you clean up. Sometimes they might even help remove the classroom holiday decorations for you.

You determine how much participation you need from parents. The upper elementary students might want to take a more active role by participating in preparations (e.g., voting on refreshments and entertainment, bringing in food, drinks, and other supplies). If you guide them in their decisions, you will be surprised at what they can do. They are also quite capable of serving the food and drinks.

Be aware that some parents may send in refreshments or favors that have not been requested. Be sure to accept these graciously and include them with the planned items so that the children involved will not experience hurt feelings. An overabundance of goodies or eats that have not been consumed can easily be dispensed by providing each child a large, plastic food storage bag to carry the extra treats home.

Be sure to allow enough time for party activities, which students eagerly anticipate. You may want to include a classroom game, holiday-related songs, or a holiday-related story. At the Valentine's Day party, you'll need to allow time for opening and discussing valentines. Remind students that they must clean up before refreshments can be served.

Finally, special plans need to be made for the party at the end of the year. If the event is held outdoors, you'll need many parents to help. If it is a grade-level party, then parents from each classroom can work together. Some grade levels plan cookouts. If this is your plan, you will need parents to cook, pour drinks, hand out food, and clean up. Remember to send home a special newsletter explaining the event and include a supply list that specifies what each student is responsible for bringing.

Careful planning for each party allows you and the children to spend a relaxed and enjoyable time together.

Form 6.1

Conference Request Form

Name: _____

Date: _____

Time: _____

I hope to see you there!

- -

Please tear off and return.

Name: _____   *Conference Date:* _____

_____ *Yes, I will be there.*

_____ *No, I cannot attend. Please reschedule another day.*

_____ *Please plan a telephone conference.*

Phone number: _____

Form 6.2

Conference Reminder Form

Just a reminder that we have a conference planned.

For: _____

Date: _____

Time: _____

Location: _____

I am looking forward to meeting with you to discuss your child's progress.

Conference Reminder Form

Just a reminder that we have a conference planned.

For: _____

Date: _____

Time: _____

Location: _____

I am looking forward to meeting with you to discuss your child's progress.

Form 6.3

Primary Conference Form

School: _____ **Date:** _____

Type of Conference:

_____ Person to person _____ Phone _____ E-mail _____ Mail

Note to parents: Thank you for attending this conference to discuss your child's education! I hope that you leave here knowing that the very best results will only come when teachers and parents work together. The best education comes from the child's surroundings in school and home, along with the surrounding community and travel experiences!

Student's Name: _____ **Student ID #:** _____

Home Address: _____

Home Phone: _____ **Grade:** _____

Parents' Names: _____ **Work #:** _____

_____ **Work #:** _____

<u>**Reading & Language Arts Instructional Level:**</u>

Above grade level _____ On grade level _____ Below grade level _____

Name of book or material used: _____

<u>**Math Instructional Level:**</u>

Above grade level _____ On grade level _____ Below grade level _____

Name of book or material used: _____

Form 6.3 (continued)

Work Habits, Behavior, Peer Relationships

E (Exceptional)   *S (Satisfactory)*   *NI (Needs Improvement)*

_____ Displays good listening skills   _____ Displays good attendance

_____ Shows effort   _____ Shows concern for others

_____ Respects others' property   _____ Is punctual

_____ Follows directions   _____ Maintains a positive attitude

_____ Completes classwork on time   _____ Completes homework on time

_____ Turns in neat work   _____ Works well in groups

_____ Accepts rules and limits   _____ Socializes at appropriate times

_____ Maintains good relationships   _____ Displays good motor skills

_____ Works independently   _____ Is self-confident

Special programs: _____

Referred to school staffing team for: _____

Potential retainee: _____

Suggestions:

_____

_____

_____

_____

Signatures of Participants (does not indicate agreement or disagreement with contents):

Teacher   Parent(s) or Guardian

_____   _____

Form 6.3 (continued)

Standardized Test Scores

Above grade level _____   On grade level _____   Below grade level _____

Name of standard test used: _____

Standardized Test Results

September

	Expected Score			Expected Score			Expected Score
Reading ___ ___			Math ___ ___			Writing ___ ___	

January

Reading ___ ___			Math ___ ___			Writing ___ ___	

Areas of Concern:

Reading ___   Math ___   Writing ___

Science / Health ___   Social Studies ___   Social / Behavior ___

Comments: _____
_____
_____
_____
_____
_____
_____

Form 6.4

Intermediate Conference Form

School: _____ Date: _____

Type of Conference:

____ Person to person ____ Phone ____ E-mail ____ Mail

Note to parents: *Thank you for attending this conference to discuss your child's education! I hope that you leave here knowing that the very best results will only come when teachers and parents work together. The best education comes from the child's surroundings in school and home, along with the surrounding community and travel experiences!*

Part I: Student Information

Student's Name: _____ Student ID #: _____

Home Address: _____

Home Phone: _____ Grade: _____

Parents' Names _____ Work #: _____

_____ Work #: _____

Part II: Academic Information

Reading & Language Arts Instructional Level:

Above grade level _____ On grade level _____ Below grade level _____

Name of book or material used: _____

Math Instructional Level:

Above grade level _____ On grade level _____ Below grade level _____

Name of book or material used: _____

Form 6.4 (continued)

Work Habits, Behavior, Peer Relationships

E (Exceptional)   *S (Satisfactory)*   *NI (Needs Improvement)*

_____ Displays good listening skills   _____ Displays good attendance

_____ Shows effort   _____ Shows concern for others

_____ Respects others' property   _____ Is punctual

_____ Follows directions   _____ Maintains a positive attitude

_____ Completes classwork on time   _____ Completes homework on time

_____ Turns in neat work   _____ Works well in groups

_____ Accepts rules and limits   _____ Socializes at appropriate times

_____ Maintains good relationships   _____ Displays good motor skills

_____ Works independently   _____ Is self-confident

Suggestions: _____
_____
_____
_____
_____

Parent has agreed to help at home by: _____
_____
_____
_____
_____

Signatures of Participants (does not indicate agreement or disagreement with contents):

Teacher   Parent(s) or Guardian

_____   _____

Form 6.4 (continued)

<u>**Standardized Test Results**</u>

September

	Expected Score		Expected Score		Expected Score
Reading ___ ___		Math ___ ___		Writing ___ ___	

January

Reading ___ ___   Math ___ ___   Writing ___ ___

<u>**Areas of Concern:**</u>

Reading ___   Math ___   Writing ___

Science / Health ___   Social Studies ___   Social / Behavior ___

Special programs: _____

Referred to school staffing team for: _____

Potential retainee: _____

Comments: _____
_____
_____
_____
_____
_____
_____
_____

Suggestions: _____
_____
_____
_____
_____

7

Making Progress Report Cards Easier

Report Card Basics

When it comes to report cards, using organizational skills can save you time and stress and will reduce the chances of making serious errors. Before you get started, do a few things to help yourself save time throughout the year and ensure that each child receives his or her own report card. For example, write the students' names on their card and arrange the cards in alphabetical order. Then, starting with the first card, write a numeral in the top left corner of each card, beginning with numeral 1. Now, whenever the cards are out of order, you will be able to quickly rearrange them.

Next, put the same numeral from the report cards on the top left corner of the report card's envelope. One reason for doing this is so you can double-check to make sure that the numbers on the report cards match the numbers on the envelopes. This helps you make sure the report card gets into the correct matching envelope. If a student were to receive the wrong report card, it could be a detrimental and humiliating experience.

Report Card Comments

Comments on report cards not only explain the child's progress, but they also tell the parents about their child's teacher. It is important to have a well-written, clear message that will help guide the parents in their child's education. It is always advisable to start with a positive comment, but if there is a problem, most parents will be grateful to you for telling them and will want to help you correct it as soon as possible. Many problems that show up at school are also problems noticed at home, so your comments will not surprise parents. Ideally, at some point prior to receiving the progress report, parents have already discussed the problem with you.

Most report cards have only a small space for comments. Therefore, it is important to decide which strengths and weaknesses you want to include.

Some teachers think by the time report cards need to be done they know their students well enough to write a quick comment. However, it is important that you be able to back up any statement that you make. Remember, you are accountable for all of the report card's details.

One way to accumulate accurate and specific comments is to observe your class and make notes, beginning a couple weeks before report cards are due to go home. One way to save time when writing notes is to use a code, such as the following, to denote the areas of improvement.

L = **L**istening

RH = **R**aising **H**and

FD = **F**ollowing **D**irections

T = Staying on **T**ask

SS = **S**chool **S**upplies

HW = **H**ome**w**ork

HFO = Using **H**ands, **F**eet, or **O**bjects to disturb others

M = **M**anners

(*Note:* For primary grades, this code is to be used by teachers only. However, in the upper grades, the code could be posted in the classroom. Line up a notebook with a page assigned to each student. At the end of each school day, place a sticky note with the appropriate codes on the designated page.)

Review your codes and notes from the past few weeks to determine who needs improvement and in what areas. It might be a student is struggling in an academic area or it could be a behavioral or attendance problem. Think of well-thought out comments for the types of needs your students may have. You will probably find that one comment can be used for several students. Always check your writing and spelling and make sure it sounds correct. If you are not sure of the spelling of a certain word, look it up in the dictionary. You might even ask a team teacher to double-check your comments.

Group your students' report cards according to the categories listed. Now write your final comments on each student's report card. You will not only have great comments, but you will also have saved yourself time agonizing over each report card.

If you are using a computer, consider typing and printing your comments on sticker labels, so if a report card is lost, you still have the comments on file. You can even copy and paste comments, changing the student's name each time, if a certain comment fits several of your students. You will be surprised how easily and quickly you can finish your report cards while still doing a competent job.

What Should My Comments Say?

Always tell something positive to parents first then tell about your concerns. Starting with problems puts parents on the defensive immediately. Leading with the positive, however, shows you appreciate their child. The following is an example of a positive comment:

> I am enjoying having Sarah in my class. She appears to have adjusted nicely to ＿＿ grade. She loves to read and is very creative in her writing. However, I am concerned about her progress in math. It would be helpful for her to practice addition and subtraction math facts for a few extra minutes each day. I will continue to monitor her progress and keep you informed. (Note: If you feel a conference is necessary at this time, you can request one.)

If you notice someone in your class is not working hard, make note of it. Watch for improvement, and if the child doesn't seem to be making progress, the comment might sound like this:

> Jimmy appears to have adjusted nicely to ＿＿ grade. He was working hard and doing well until about two weeks ago, when I noticed that he stopped caring about the quality of his work. I will continue to monitor and encourage him to work harder in class. It would be helpful if you could also be watchful at home with his homework.

It is important that you include the parents in your comment, so they know the child's education is a joint mission.

Sometimes you need to sound firm so that parents know you need their help and that you will not allow their child to continue inappropriate behavior. Such a comment might sound like this:

> Jennifer appears to enjoy _____ grade. However, I am concerned with her talking out and interrupting during class. Please address this problem with her. I will continue to monitor her in class. I know she could improve academically if she listened more and talked less. Thank you for your help.

For a student who can't seem to get along with anyone and always blames others, the comment might be written like this:

> Joey is showing academic progress in all areas. However, I am concerned with his social skills. He needs to accept responsibility for his own actions, without blaming others. Please talk with him about this problem. I would like to schedule a conference, so we can discuss together how to meet his needs.

If your comment asks for a conference, schedule one and put a conference slip in the report card envelope. The child may need additional help from the school psychologist or guidance counselor; you can ask the school psychologist or guidance counselor to sit in on the conference, so he or she can help brainstorm ideas with the parents.

You will usually have a student who is having trouble academically and cannot focus. You need to address this problem and get the parent involved. In this situation, your comment might be written like this:

> Emma seems to enjoy _____ grade and is very kind to her peers. However, I have noticed that she is having trouble focusing on her work. Because of this, she is struggling academically in all her subjects. I would like to meet with you and discuss some ideas that I have to try to help Emma feel more successful.

Again, a conference slip should go home with the report card. You might need to get the school nurse involved and spend time observing the child before meeting with the parents. The nurse can help set up a medical checkup to determine the child's needs.

The comments on the first report card are usually the most difficult. At the second or third grading period, you will merely add whether the child is improving or is still showing a lack of progress. Comments on later report cards might look like this:

> Sarah continues to do well in language arts. Since our last conference, I have noticed improved progress in her math due to your invaluable help at home. Keep up the good work!

> During this grading period, Jimmy has shown definite improvement in the quality of his work. Thank you for your encouragement and support in helping me with this problem.

If improvement is not evident, you might write a comment such as the following:

> During this grading period, Jorge has shown the desire to improve the quality of his work. However, he continues to have difficulty in this area. I have noticed that the quality and quantity of his work is affected by his poor handwriting. I would like to discuss this with you in further detail. (Please see conference slip for time.)

Cassie has shown academic improvement this quarter and has curtailed her talking somewhat since her seat was changed. However, I would greatly appreciate your continued support in dealing with this problem.

Sometimes it is necessary to lower a student's grade. If this should happen, your comment should reflect the reason for your decision, and you should be ready to back it up with documentation.

Brian still relates well to his peers and appears to continue to enjoy school. However, I was disappointed in his test scores in math and reading. The scores clearly show that he is not putting forth the effort needed. I would like to discuss this with you, so we determine how best to help him.

Communicating competently on a report card is essential to maintaining the cooperation of parents. Report cards should reflect your professionalism, your caring attitude, and your understanding of each child.

You will need to be clear about the child's problem, being *kind* but *firm* in your comments. When you have a child in your class who displays disruptive behavior, make sure you have documentation of the child's actions. Be ready to sit down with parents who may pop in after school unannounced to discuss their child's problem. Keep your notes in a handy folder, so you have something to jog your memory. Teachers who are not prepared can be intimidated by such parents and find it hard after a long day in the classroom to recall specific situations. Lack of documentation makes the parents think that you are unclear about the situation and that you are picking on their child.

8

End-of-the-Year Planning Tips

You are approaching the last month of the end of the year. All of a sudden everything seems to be coming due (report cards, cumulative folders, textbook inventories, and classroom and art order forms). You are still expected to continue teaching and end-of-the-year testing. This is definitely the time to sit down, plan, and pace yourself.

Getting Started

Start early and anticipate what you need to do and when each task needs to be done. Mark due dates on your calendar. Now plan your strategy to get it all done.

There are many things you can do to help prepare yourself. First, look for a reliable volunteer. About five weeks before school is out, have this person straighten your bookcases and cupboards while taking inventory of your art and school supplies. Later, when it comes time to make your supply list for fall, you will know what to order.

Next, ask your volunteer to help put away your bulletin boards, manipulatives, and any teaching items you will not need. The volunteer can even organize the items you will need for the beginning of the next school year, so they will be ready when you come back in the fall.

Some teachers even have their volunteers put up their bulletin boards for the upcoming fall events during the last week of school. If you cover them with newspaper, they won't get dirty when the custodians clean during the summer.

If your school has a clerical aide to copy papers for teachers, use this person wisely at this time of year. If possible, have the aide copy about three weeks of spelling lists, math problems, and homework, or any other papers you will need during the first weeks of the next school year. Look back at your lesson plans for the first weeks of school and let those be your guide. You will be thankful when you return in the fall because the beginning of school offers little time to copy papers, and everyone will want to use the copy machine.

This is a good time to start collecting boxes and storing them for later packing. Paper boxes are sturdy and a nice size for storage. You don't want boxes that are too large because they are too difficult to move. You will also need packing tape and permanent markers to seal and label the boxes. In the boxes, pack items such as your classroom library books, dictionaries, manipulatives, puzzles, games, and so on.

As the textbook inventory approaches, ask your volunteer to help you. Use the checklist to determine which books are missing and be sure to give students time to look for them. Send out the Missing Book Notice (Form 8.1) to any student who is missing a book so that his or her parents can get involved. After the inventory, when all books are accounted for, your volunteer can put the books away. (See the lost book letter at the end of this chapter.)

Have your volunteer help you dust, pack up your computer center, and clean and organize other centers, so they will be ready for the next school year. The end of the year requires a lot of cleaning, ordering, and organization. With a little planning and help, you can save yourself a lot of stress. As a token of your appreciation, give your volunteer a small gift.

Additional Tips

- When you have finished your order for school and art supplies, make sure you keep a copy in your records, so you can double-check the items when they come in. Keep this copy in a safe place, where it will be readily available the next fall.

- Create an end-of-year checklist for things that need to be done. Start with the more difficult chores. As you complete each job, check it off. This way you know at all times what still needs to be done.

- Check early with one of your team teachers on how to complete your students' cumulative folders. Each school has its own procedure, and it is important to follow it exactly.

- Ask your volunteer if he or she would be available the first week of school to help you reorganize your classroom. Since the volunteer helped put items away, he or she will most likely remember where they are.

- On one of the last days of school, leave a drawing or pictures on the chalkboard showing how you would like your classroom to be set up. This will help the custodians to know how to arrange your furniture after your room has been cleaned. Label all bookcases, tables, and desks according to the labels in your drawing.

Form 8.1

Lost Book Notice

Dear Parent(s)/Guardian(s),

    This letter is to inform you that your child, _____, has

(name)

lost, misplaced, defaced, or ruined his/her _____ textbook,

(circle the appropriate one)

no. _____. He/she was assigned the book to use and to care for during the

(subject)

school year of _____. If it is not returned by _____, then

(year)   (date)

he/she will be held responsible for the cost of this book. The replacement cost

of this textbook is _____. Please look at home or in any other place that this book

(amount)

may be found. The school system tracks all textbooks, and it is important that every

child have the opportunity to have a book to use during the school year.

    Thank you for understanding and complying with our policy. Please remit

the amount noted above and include the tear-off portion of this note with your

remittance.

_____, Teacher

- -

Please accept this _____ for the replacement cost of

(amount)

_____'s _____ textbook, no. _____.

(name of student)

Sincerely,

_____, Parent/Guardian

(parent/guardian signature)

9

No Child Left Behind

In 2002, President George W. Bush signed into law the No Child Left Behind Act. This act is the most thorough educational reform since The Elementary and Secondary Act (ESEA) of 1965. No Child Left Behind (NCLB) redefines the role of our federal government in K–12 education. Its main purpose is to close the achievement gap between minority and disadvantaged students and their peers. In other words, no child shall be left behind.

This act is based on four principles:

1. There will be increased flexibility and more local (state and district) control.

2. There will be expanded options for parents of minorities or disadvantaged students.

3. There will be better and stronger accountability for achievement results.

4. There will be an emphasis on using certain teaching methods that have been proven to work.

In this chapter, we take each of these four principles and discuss how each affects you as a professional educator. Remember, it is your responsibility to do your best to encourage each child to achieve his or her highest potential.

Flexibility

NCLB mandates that states and local school districts be given more input and flexibility as to the kinds of programs they need and how they spend federal money. Most states now have, or will have, certain educational standards, or goals, that each school district within the state must use to guide their curriculum. In turn, each school district is expected to set certain benchmarks in their curriculum that directly relate to these state standards. This allows the curriculum to be more uniform throughout all schools. Assessments are given at certain grade levels to measure the achievement of these benchmarks.

You must make yourself aware of these state standards and instruct your students according to the benchmarks for your particular grade level. Some textbooks include the benchmarks in their teacher manuals. Many school districts also provide curriculum guidelines, which include the benchmarks. Be aware of which skills are tested and include enough practice for your students to achieve success. It is a good idea to review the scores after each assessment and identify the specific skills your students have not mastered. That way, you will know which concepts need more emphasis, before the next test. These assessment results tell you how you are doing as a teacher. Good teachers always search for ways to improve instruction, and vary their instructional approach to teach difficult concepts before they are tested.

Accountability

NCLB also calls for stronger accountability results. This means that not only will standards be set, but also there will be stricter consequences for the results. The process of accountability includes constantly measuring how we are doing and taking responsibility for the outcome.

You must be aware of when certain assessments will be given to your students and prepare them accordingly. Follow your school district's guidelines closely to ensure that you are on the right track. You may find that you must conduct more informal assessments to know whether your students are fully prepared for the test. This takes work on your part! Sometimes it is easier for teacher grade-level teams to get together and make up a preliminary assessment for the students.

Let your students see their results individually. It is not a good idea to share the results in front of the entire class using individual names and scores because students with low scores will be uncomfortable. Instead, make up a code by giving each student his or her own letter or number combination. Put the results (in code) on graphs whenever possible and post these in the classroom. In some cases, students can graph their own results and keep them handy to compare to their next score. Discuss these graphs with your students and refer to them often. Talk about what it will take to improve these scores. In other words, let your students "buy into" the results, which allows them to become more active learners.

Share the assessment results with parents, too. They should know where their child's strengths and weaknesses are because they can often be helpful at home. Others may decide to get special help for their child, such as tutoring. By keeping your students and parents involved in the learning process, you are making them a part of the educational team. A student who is given enough guidance and support will generally be one of the higher scoring ones. Success is best accomplished through team effort.

Parental Options

NCLB provides expanded options for parents, requiring each school district to keep a list of state-approved services for children, such as tutoring classes, after-school and summer classes, remedial help, and special services. It also requires that each state set the standards, or goals, that every school must meet. Schools that do not make adequate progress for two consecutive years will be identified as needing improvement.

Charter School Provisions

This act also encourages more parental options through the use of certain charter schools. Theoretically, charter schools are public schools that are free to use innovation to provide more efficient programs, and charter schools usually have been identified and deemed successful at improving academic achievement through the use of these programs. Students attending schools identified as poor performing are given the option to go to any of the public or charter schools available.

Proven Teaching Methodologies

The fourth basic principle of NCLB pertains especially to teachers. It puts an emphasis on the use of teaching methods that have been proven to work. Teach First, the entity that defined these methods and has put several programs into action, has identified elementary literacy as the most important link to academic improvement. All of the Teach First teaching strategies, or methods, have been established by the National Staff Development Council, have been validated through research as successful strategies, and have been proven to work in actual classrooms, with real students, who are taught by certified teachers.

Key Strategies

The following list contains proven strategies identified as essential to improving literacy by Teach First council:

- Phonemic awareness

- Phonics

- Read alouds

- Shared reading

- Independent reading

- Modeled writing

- Shared writing

- Guided writing

- Independent writing

- Comprehension skills

- Reading and writing across the curriculum

Teach First also addresses limited English proficiency (LEP) students and immigrants. It provides for research-validated and proven strategies for LEP students through mentoring and professional support for new teachers.

As a new or inexperienced teacher, you should be aware of the Teach First program. If your school or district has a significant number of LEP students or immigrants, then it would benefit you to become involved in this program. The program calls for mentor teachers, guest speakers, and continuing education courses to help classroom teachers develop successful strategies to teach LEP students.

All professional teachers and school districts should be aware of NCLB. Many districts throughout North America use the Teach First program to help inexperienced teachers develop effective teaching strategies and work toward continued success in the classroom. The Teach First Web site offers many ideas and practical suggestions for teachers (www.teachfirst.com).

Today's teacher should be up-to-date on the kinds of teaching methods that work best for students to enhance the child's learning experience and comprehension. Additionally, by being aware of the support systems available and the latest proven teaching strategies, you ensure your effectiveness as a teacher, leading to a long and successful career. (Please see "Latest Teaching Tips and Strategies" later in this chapter for more activities that support the Teach First council's strategies.)

Learning Style Theories and How to Incorporate Them Into Your Instruction

It is known that children learn by different methods, but there are many theories as to how the actual learning process takes place. No doubt, if you have attended an accredited college or university, you have been exposed to several of these learning style theories. We briefly touch on a few of them in this book, but our main purpose is to review these theories and help guide you while you make lesson plans. Make sure that you include various methods and strategies when introducing new material to your students; doing so allows you to cover the curriculum in a number of different ways.

The VAK Theory

One of the earliest learning style theories is the VAK, or the *Visual* learner, the *Auditory* learner, and the *Kinesthetic* learner. According to this theory, all students learn in all three of these ways, but usually one way is more predominant.

Students who learn better *visually* learn by seeing concepts in print, by writing concepts down, or by reading about concepts. These students often recall information that is written, even though they may have only read it once. Many of these learners do well using graphs, charts, outlines, illustrations, written notes, printed study sheets, and so on.

On the other hand, students whose predominant style of learning is through *auditory* channels will probably learn best through class discussion, teacher lectures, or conversations with a partner. These students work well while listening to tape-recorded lessons. For these students, it's a good idea to begin a lesson with a brief explanation of what is coming and review with a summary of what has been covered.

The last type of learner is the *kinesthetic* learner. Student who learn this way learns by moving around and touching things. This is called the hands-on approach, and every elementary teacher should include many of these learning activities in their daily lessons. Singing songs, dancing, playing music, acting out a skit, using highlighters while reading, transferring text to a keyboard, using colored markers, drawing pictures, or using math manipulatives, such as markers, coins, string, rulers, tape, shapes, balls, and so forth, all help kinesthetic learners master concepts.

Kolb's Theory

Kolb's theory on learning styles is based on the experiences that one has. Kolb states that learners (through their experiences) absorb information in either a concrete or a reflective manner. The concrete learner learns best by being actively involved in new experiences—in other words, they learn by doing, or being directly involved in a process. On the other hand, reflective learners learn best by observing others in the experiment or by developing their own observations through experimentation. By giving your students the chance to be involved in experiments, all students—both the concrete and the reflective learners—benefit. A teacher can provide these opportunities through the use of hands-on activities, such as the following examples:

- Classroom journals or logs
- Laboratories

- Field exercises and observations

- Group brainstorming

- Teamwork activities

- Homework assignments that encourage these types of activities

Be sure that your lesson plans incorporate a variety of these activities. You may feel uncomfortable doing some of these activities with your students at first because interaction can be noisy, and traditional teachers may not be used to this. You will probably find that as you do more of them, you become more comfortable. Seeing your students actively involved in the learning process is a reward in itself.

Gardner's Multiple Intelligence Theory

Howard Gardner's theory of multiple intelligences is based on the idea that, in our culture, the school systems teach and assess only two kinds of intelligences—verbal and linguistic. The theory of multiple intelligences provides for at least seven other kinds of intelligences, which are equally important. The other kinds of intelligences include visual/spatial, body/kinesthetic, musical, interpersonal, intrapersonal, and nature. His theory suggests that even more forms may be realized in the future. Children in our schools should be exposed every day to environments that address each one of these forms of intelligence so that students can reach each individual's fullest potential.

From these various theories we recognize that each of us learns in a preferred way. If new concepts are presented to us in a manner that allows us to best integrate them into our minds, then we learn at a faster rate and are better prepared to face the future. Teachers must always be aware that people do learn in different ways and must try to include many strategies and techniques in student lessons. To help you with this, we have provided you with some of the most recent tips and strategies.

Latest Reading Tips and Strategies

This partial list of instructional methods should be included in your lesson plans. If you use some of each of these in your weekly lessons, then you will be most successful in reaching each student through his or her own preferred learning style.

- *Peer Tutors*—Let two or three children work on an assignment together. It is most beneficial if one student is more knowledgeable in the subject. Try not to put two weaker students together.

- *Buddy Reading*—Let your students read aloud together in pairs. Talk about using good "buddy reading manners" before they attempt this activity. Make sure they understand that they are to help each other when needed. Try to pair a low-performing child with one who is more capable.

- *Phonetics*—Phonetics is the study of linguistic sounds, how they are produced (articulatory phonetics), how they are perceived (auditory or perceptual phonetics), and their physical aspects (acoustic phonetics). Phonemes are a basic sound elements system on which to build future vocabulary.

- *Teacher Read Aloud*—Children who are read to develop good listening skills, a love of the printed word, and the desire to learn to read.

- *Independent Reading*—Children should be encouraged to not only be read to but also to enjoy reading independently. Independent readers should be able to find a quiet area in the classroom to concentrate on the written word.

- *Model Writing*—In this activity, the teacher generates with the students ideas on how to put words into an interesting piece of writing which might include a topic sentence, several supporting sentences, and a good ending. The teacher models how to space the words, how to use capital letters and punctuation correctly, how to sound out words while writing, and how to check to make sure the writing makes sense.

- *Guided Writing*—In guided writing, students write independently, working on stories or writing in their journals. The teacher walks around the room, observing, commenting, and noting writing mistakes for future minilessons.

- *Reading and Writing Across the Curriculum*—Many teachers like to teach units that integrate all subjects. In this type of literacy activity, the students' writing reflects what they learned and how it relates to all subject areas.

- *Graphic Organizers*—Word/vocabulary webs, story maps, diagrams, lists, Venn diagrams, and other organizers give many students a better understanding of a lesson or greater comprehension of a story or article.

- *Manipulatives*—Flash cards, number and place value charts, games, songs or rhymes, puzzles, informational posters, cubes, calculators, and overhead projector pieces, among other manipulatives, help enhance math lessons and other concepts.

- *Teacher Monitoring*—After introducing a lesson and assigning a practice activity, the teacher should circulate around the room, observing the students and assisting them when needed.

- *Cooperative Learning*—Be sure to give students time every day to work cooperatively. Children are almost always naturally social, and this allows them the opportunity to learn through social interaction. Second language learners, international students, and those with disabilities especially gain from this type of activity.

- *Lesson Review*—Include frequent reviews of concepts taught. Have the children summarize what they have learned or read. They can do this in writing, or they can present their summaries to the class using visual aids.

- *Comprehension Discussions*—Class or group discussions held after reading a story or an article enhance your students' comprehension. Have four or five students work as a team in literacy circles or groups to read and discuss their assignments.

- *Word Walls*—Also called word banks, this strategy uses one wall or bulletin board as a vocabulary wall. As each new word is introduced, it is added to the word wall. Review the words frequently and refer to the wall as the words are repeatedly used. Encourage students to use these words in their writing.

- *Problem-Solving Methods*—Hang posters in the classroom that illustrate the problem-solving sequence and strategies. After discussing and practicing each strategy, use them as appropriate throughout the year. When students are given a problem-solving task, ask them to point out and explain which method they used to solve it.

- *Teacher of the Day*—Give each student the opportunity to be the teacher for a particular lesson or review. This gives students the opportunity to be in front of their peers while summarizing a concept previously learned. Being in front of the class gives them the chance to feel important. Another option is to let them pretend they are producing a TV learning show.

- *Shared Writing*—Students should be encouraged to share their writing daily. Time will not allow all of your students to share each day, but be sure to have a daily sharing time. A good way to keep track of which students have or have not shared is to put each child's name on the end of an ice cream stick. Place two large plastic drinking cups on a small table near the front of the room. Label one cup "Not Shared" and the other "Shared." After a child shares his or her story for the week, place the child's stick into the "Shared" cup. This helps keep track of who has shared and who has not. Some students enjoy sharing, and others would rather not share. Encourage students to share at least once each week, even if their stories are incomplete. Always encourage the writer by having others tell something that they liked about the story, then slowly work into some constructive suggestions.

- *Student Leaders*—Give students the opportunity to be a leader in the classroom. If you place desks in groups of four or five, you can assign one student in each group to be student leader. Otherwise, select a leader for each row. These students can be responsible for handing out and collecting papers for the group. Also, you can appoint group monitors. When the group is working on a project, it is the monitor's job to remind other students in the group to talk quietly, take turns, and work together. Or, if students are sent to the library in groups, the group monitor reminds his or her group to walk quietly to and from the library.

Additional Resources

The NCLB has a special Web site for parents who want to become more involved with their children's education but don't know exactly what to do. For more detailed information, visit the U.S. Department of Education Web site (www.ed.gov/nclb/). Here parents will find a set of publications titled "Helping Your Child Series," which will help them support their children. This series includes booklets that can be downloaded, including the following titles:

- "Helping Your Child Become a Reader"

- "Helping Your Child with Homework"

- "Helping Your Preschool Child"

- "Helping Your Child Succeed in School"

- "Helping Your Child through Early Adolescence"

The Web site also provides a Webcast series for parents and a link to education-related news. This information is worthwhile, especially for parents who are willing but unsure of how to help with their child's education.

It would help you to be aware of these and other resources (e.g., other educational Web sites, educational supply stores, private tutors, extra worksheets, learning games) that may be helpful to some of your students' parents. You are the expert, so give useful suggestions and advice freely. Not every parent is knowledgeable enough to know where to go for help. You could provide this information during parent-teacher conferences, during Open House, or through a classroom newsletter or Web site.

State-Mandated Tests versus Teacher-Directed Lessons

Many states now have state-mandated tests that are given at certain grade levels. If your state does not, then the students probably are given one or more of the well-known basic skills tests, such as the Stanford Achievement Tests (SAT) or the Iowa Test of Basic Skills (ITBS). These tests are used to compare the progress of a certain group of students to national standings.

These annual tests can cause instruction-related concerns for teachers. Teachers are expected to cover all of the skills in each of the grade-level subjects. This goal in itself is a daunting task! Teaching extra skills for the test just adds more responsibility to already overburdened educators. Teachers must maintain a balance of test-related and curriculum-related lessons within their classrooms. Most educators agree that there are certain skills or concepts that are necessary and worthy but that may not be included in the annual assessments. You must use your judgment and teach those that you feel are necessary for the future success of the students. Keep in mind that learning a wide range of skills makes students well-rounded individuals.

Techniques for Teaching Writing

You have just finished your curriculum courses in college and are ready to start teaching. Now what do you do, and how do you get started? Two excellent books you might consider for your personal use are . . . *And with a Light Touch* by Carol Avery, and *The Art of Teaching Writing* by Lucy McCormick Calkins. Both books have great ideas to help you get off to a great start and make you feel more comfortable teaching writing.

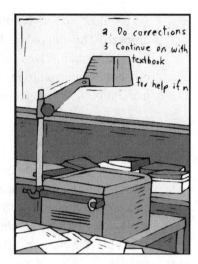

Many standardized tests now have several parts that are written. Parts of the math section might ask a student to "explain your strategy in finding your answer." Also, many of the tests have a writing part to check the students' skill in expressing themselves through writing. This next section will help you with ideas on how to prepare students through writing. NCLB watches for improvement in this area each year through testing to make sure all students are reading and writing up to the standards.

Teaching children good writing techniques is difficult for some teachers, especially for those who do not enjoy writing themselves. Some people seem to possess a natural ability for writing stories and articles, while others struggle to get a few words on paper. A teacher who encourages everyone to write creatively gives his or her students a lasting and useful gift.

First, you must be dedicated to having your students write every day. This writing could be in the form of a writer's workshop, held for a period of 15 to 20 minutes each day, or it could be in the form of written assignments. Writing should also be frequently included in homework assignments, and regular writing minilessons should be taught. Minilessons should cover a number of different techniques and writing strategies. During minilessons, demonstrate to students your respect for the written word by sharing some phrases or paragraphs that you feel are well written. Share a variety of genres with them, from poetry to prose. Discuss words and phrases that sound particularly interesting. When reading a story to your students, stop when you come to a clever or well-written section of the story. Repeat the paragraph or section after you tell your students what you liked about it. Different authors have certain strengths; share them with your students.

Ideas to Help Get Your Students Started

One of the greatest problems young children have with writing is deciding what to write about. The following ideas will help your students select topics and begin writing.

- Start the year brainstorming together and listing different topics students can write about. Have them list the topics as they are mentioned and keep the list in their writing portfolios. Then, when they run out of writing ideas, they can refer to this list.

- Use story starters, or prompts, to help children get started writing. Type a collection of story starters on a strip of paper. Occasionally give the same story starter to everyone. It's interesting to see how many different stories students write using the same story starter.

- Make up questions or statements related to literature read in class. Have students write in response to this reading. This kind of writing gives students the opportunity to discuss their opinions about issues in the reading and life in general.

- Designate a certain time of day for journal writing. These 10 or 15 minutes should be free time for students to write about anything they choose. Journaling gives students the freedom to express themselves and their feelings.

- As a follow-up activity after taking a field trip, have students write about what they saw and enjoyed. This not only reinforces what students learned but also gives them the opportunity to express themselves freely. In other words, it's not the form they have to think of but the content. Some children find it less threatening when they don't have to worry about the organization of a composition.

Elements of a Good Composition

- *Emergent Writing*—Start teaching writing to your students even before they understand what a complete sentence is. Have them share their stories and talk about writing by using complete sentences, or thoughts. Teach this skill until you feel comfortable knowing that almost everyone in your class is capable of writing in sentences. Then move on to paragraphs. Learning the writing process in gradual steps builds a firm foundation for future school years.

- *Topic Selection*—Teach your students to think of a small, interesting topic. It's easier to enhance a simple story than one that is too full of different ideas. Teach them how to narrow down the topic. Instead of writing about their dog, Millie, have them imagine that their story might be more interesting if they narrowed it down to tell about the day that Millie ran away or when they bought Millie a collar. It's difficult for children to narrow down topics but if you give a minilesson on writing that way, some of them will try it. Have students share their stories to learn from each other. Compare the two types of stories—the broader one with the more narrow one. Occasionally, you need to write your own stories and share them. This allows students to learn topic selection, among other things, from your example.

- *Focus*—Use minilessons to teach about staying on topic. Start by reading aloud some paragraphs that have one sentence that doesn't belong with the others. Talk about the sentence being off topic. Next, read another paragraph and ask if students can detect which sentence does not belong. Have students practice by giving them a simple prompt to write a paragraph about. Share these with the class and ask if the paragraphs remain on topic.

- *Genre*—Teach your students that there are several different types of written works. Writing can be either an expository or a narrative composition. Expository compositions are those in which the writer tries to explain something—for example, an explanation of a procedure. Narrative writing tells a story. It is quite often written in chronological order, but not always. Narrative writing can be factual, or it can be entirely or partially fictional. Other writing, such as informational articles, poetry, friendly and business letters, and journals are written for other reasons. Some try to entertain the reader; others try to give information. Introduce your students to all kinds of writing. Discuss the genre and its purpose and let students try writing each kind.

- *Story Plan*—Teach students to plan their stories before they write. Explain that this is called planning, and if they plan three good parts to their story, then it will be more interesting to the reader. The three parts of the story are: the lead, which tells a reader what the writer is writing about; the middle, which has all the interesting details of the story; and the conclusion, which ties the story together. Have your students write their ideas and tell as much about each part as they can, using as many details as possible to make it more interesting. Each part of the story should begin with a new paragraph.

- *Lead Paragraph*—Gradually instruct your students in how to introduce their writing using a lead, which is a sentence or two to hook readers. Leads can be one of the following two types:

  1. *Narrative*—In narrative writing, the lead should mention the place, time, person, and topic. To make it more interesting, students could add a simile. Give a minilesson on similes before students try adding them. Ask students to look for similes in the stories they read and share them with the class. Some teachers have students keep a list of clever similes that they have encountered in their reading. When reading aloud to your students, tell them to be listening for similes. Other possible leads are starting with a setting (time and place), a sound, an action, or by opening with a sentence using your senses. Encourage your students to vary their leads.

  2. *Expository*—In expository writing, the lead could be a question directly related to the topic. For instance, if you ask your students to write about their favorite activity when they are away from school, their writing might start with "Do you enjoy feeling the gentle wind blow through your hair? Do you like nature and music, too? If you do, then I know you'll love hearing about what I do every Saturday morning. Let me tell you about roller-blading with my friends, which is my favorite activity when I have a day off from school." In expository writing, the student gives information, explains something, or clarifies an idea. Usually the questions answered are how, why, and the ordered process. Many times it gives the steps using transition words (see next page) in order to have clarity in their writing.

- *Details*—Details in a story make it interesting. In a minilesson, read from a book that is rich with details. Don't tell students what the author is describing. Have students close their eyes while you read the detailed section to them, and when you are finished reading, ask them to tell you what the author was describing. Tell students that if they find rich details in their reading to share the passage with the class. Practice writing paragraphs using details. Explain that details are the words that paint a picture in the reader's mind and let the reader feel the way the author does.

- *Conclusion*—The words at the end of the story should let the reader know that the story has ended. The last paragraph of an expository text should summarize the main points. Quite often, a writer can reword the lead to make the ending. Tell your students that the last paragraph should sound like the end without having to write "The End." Practice writing good endings after reading some.

- *Word Usage*—Word choice can make a story great or just mediocre. Teach students to use one or two unusual words in their stories. These words should fit the situation but have a little more pizzazz than other commonly used words. Teach them not to use the same word repetitively. As you come across words that are unusual, list them on the classroom word wall. This allows students to access and use the words as the need arises. They might also keep a word list in their writing portfolio.

• *Transition Words*—Teach students to show that the story is moving through the use of transition words. Transition words help stories move on smoothly and show a connection between paragraphs. Writers should begin a new paragraph with transition words to help the reader move through the story. The following table provides common transition words.

Table 9.1   Common Transition Words

Narrative Transition Words	Expository Transition Words
First/ The first thing that happened . . .	The first reason that I chose this . . .
Second/ The second thing that . . .	The second reason that . . .
Next/ The next thing that happened . . .	The third reason . . . / The last reason . . .
Finally/ The last thing that happened . . .	Finally . . . / In conclusion . . .
Lastly/ Therefore . . . / In conclusion . . .	My advice to anyone trying this is . . .

There are many other transition words but start out with only a few until your students get used to using them. Once they understand how to use transition words, they will find others on their own.

Keep students' work in one place, in individual folders or portfolios. Keep the portfolios on a shelf and have classroom helpers pass them out when needed. Then, when you need to show them for an academic showcase night or to the parents during conferences, they will be readily available and in good condition.

Writing instruction can be very rewarding. Just relax, share your stories with your students, and teach them the joy of writing. If they learn writing can be a pleasant activity, then they will be more inclined to write. People with writing skills are able to perform well in other school subjects.

Recommended Reading

Writing Instruction

Avery, Carol. *. . . And With a Light Touch.* Portsmouth, NH: Heinemann Publishers, 1993.

Calkins, Lucy McCormick. *The Art of Teaching Writing.* Portsmouth, NH: Heinemann Publishers, 1994.

Clemmons, J., L. Laase, D. Cooper, N. Areglado, and M. Dill. *Portfolios in the Classroom—A Teacher's Sourcebook.* New York: Scholastic, Inc., 1996.

Dancing with the Pen—The Learner as a Writer. Wellington, New Zealand: Learning Media Limited, 1995.

Discipline

Albert, Linda. *A Teacher's Guide to Cooperative Discipline.* Circle Pines, MN: American Guidance Service, 1989.

Canter, L., and M. Canter. *Assertive Discipline: Positive Behavior Management for Today's Classroom.* Santa Monica, CA: Lee Canter and Associates, 1992.

Epanchin, Betty C., B. Townsend, and K. Stoddard. *Constructive Classroom Management: Strategies for Creating Positive Learning Environments.* Pacific Grove, CA: Brooks/Cole Pub. Co., 1994.

Hoppenstedt, E. M. *A Teacher's Guide to Classroom Management.* Springfield, IL: Charles C. Thomas, 1991.

Mendler, A. N. *What Do I Do When? How to Achieve Discipline with Dignity in the Classroom.* Bloomington, IN: National Educational Service, 1992.

Spaulding, C. L. *Motivation in the Classroom.* New York: McGraw-Hill, 1992.

Humor in Teaching

Hill, D. J. *School Days, Fun Days: Creative Ways to Teach Humor Skills in the Classroom.* Springfield, IL: Charles C. Thomas, 1993.

Levine, C. A. *Silly School Riddles and Other Classroom Crack-ups.* Niles, IL: A. Whitman, 1984.

Loomans, D., and K. Kolberg. *The Laughing Classroom: Everyone's Guide to Teaching with Humor and Play.* Tiburon, CA: J. Kramer, Inc., 1993.

Cooking Activities

Barchers, Suzanne I., Patricia C. Marden, and Leann Mullineaux. (Illustrator). *Cooking up U.S. History: Recipes and Research to Share with Children.* Englewood, CO: Libraries Unlimited, 1999.

Barchers, Suzanne I., and Peter J. Rauen. *Storybook Stew: Cooking with Books Kids Love.* Golden, CO: Fulcrum, 1997.

Index

About the Authors

Donna M. Donoghue, Sally Wakefield, and Esther Collins became good friends while teaching together at Sunset Hills Elementary in Tarpon Springs, Florida, and later collaborated on this book. Donna, who has taught more than 25 years, lives with her husband, Kevin, in Dunedin, Florida, and is currently teaching second grade at San Jose Elementary in Dunedin. Sally, who taught for 26 years—21 of them at Sunset Hills—retired in 2001 and also lives in Dunedin with her husband, Sarge. Esther, who taught for 38 years—31 of them at Sunset Hills—retired in 1999 and lives with her husband, Darrell, in Palm Harbor, Florida.